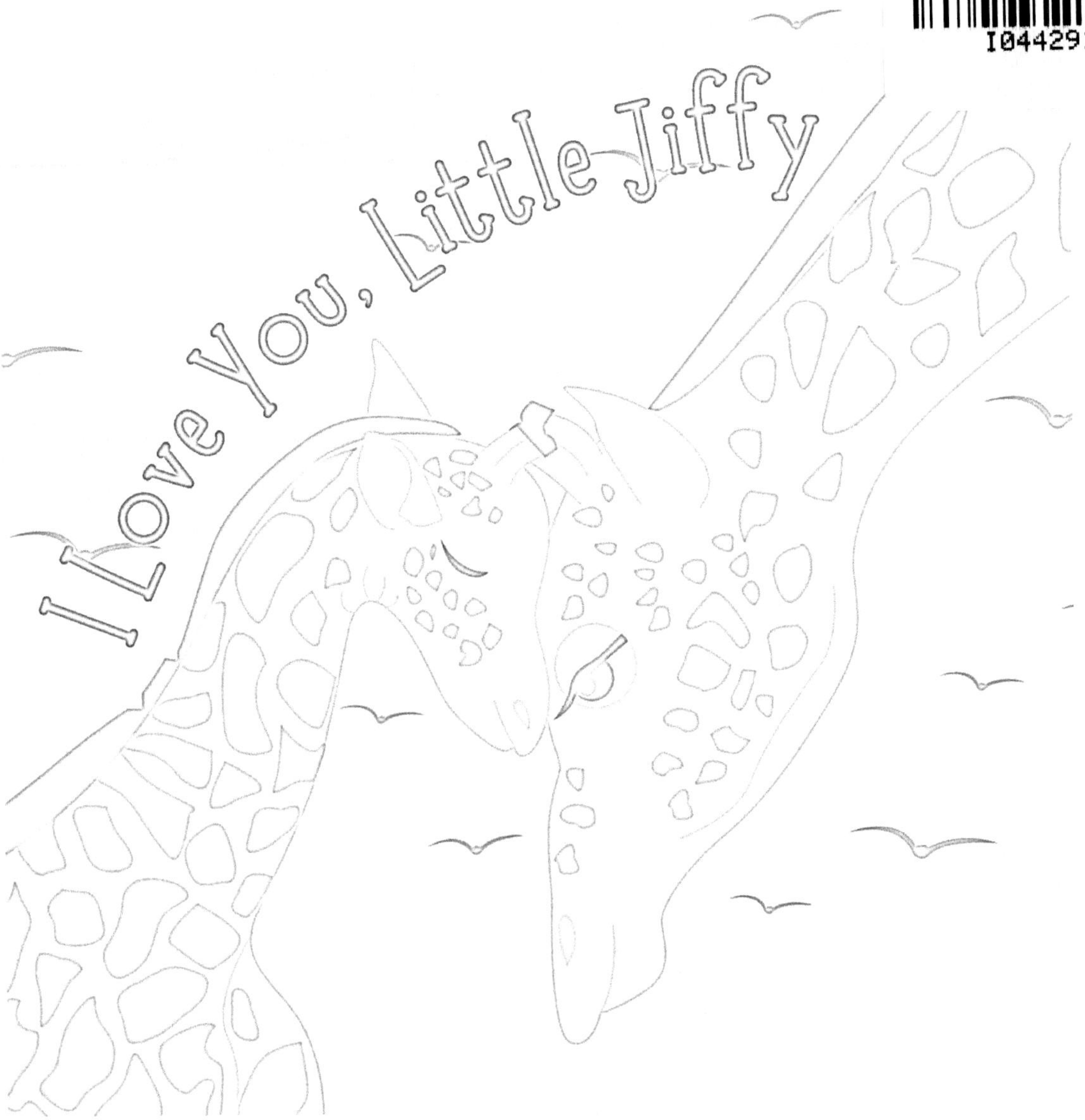

THIS COLORING BOOK BELONGS TO

____

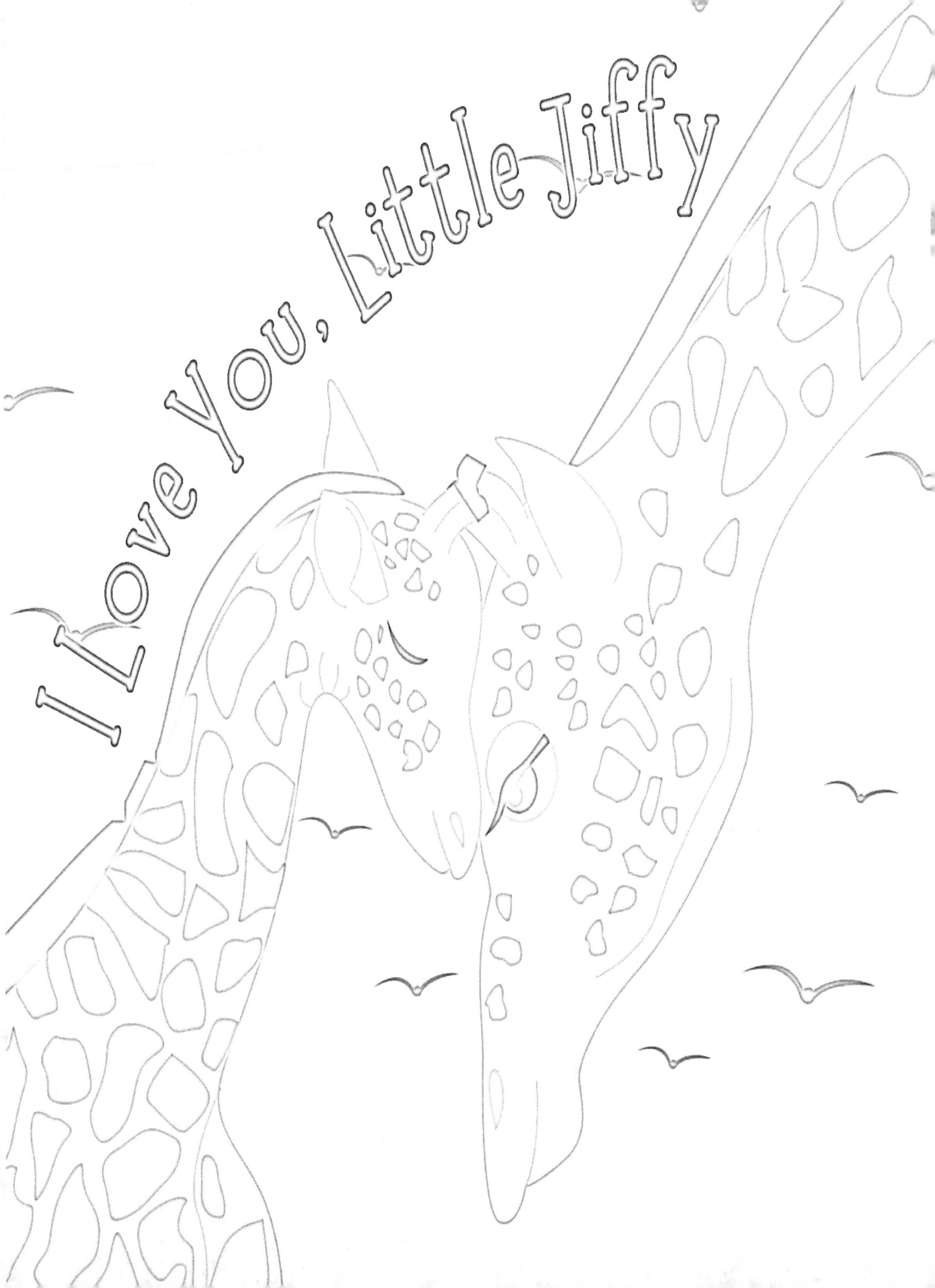
I Love You, Little Jiffy

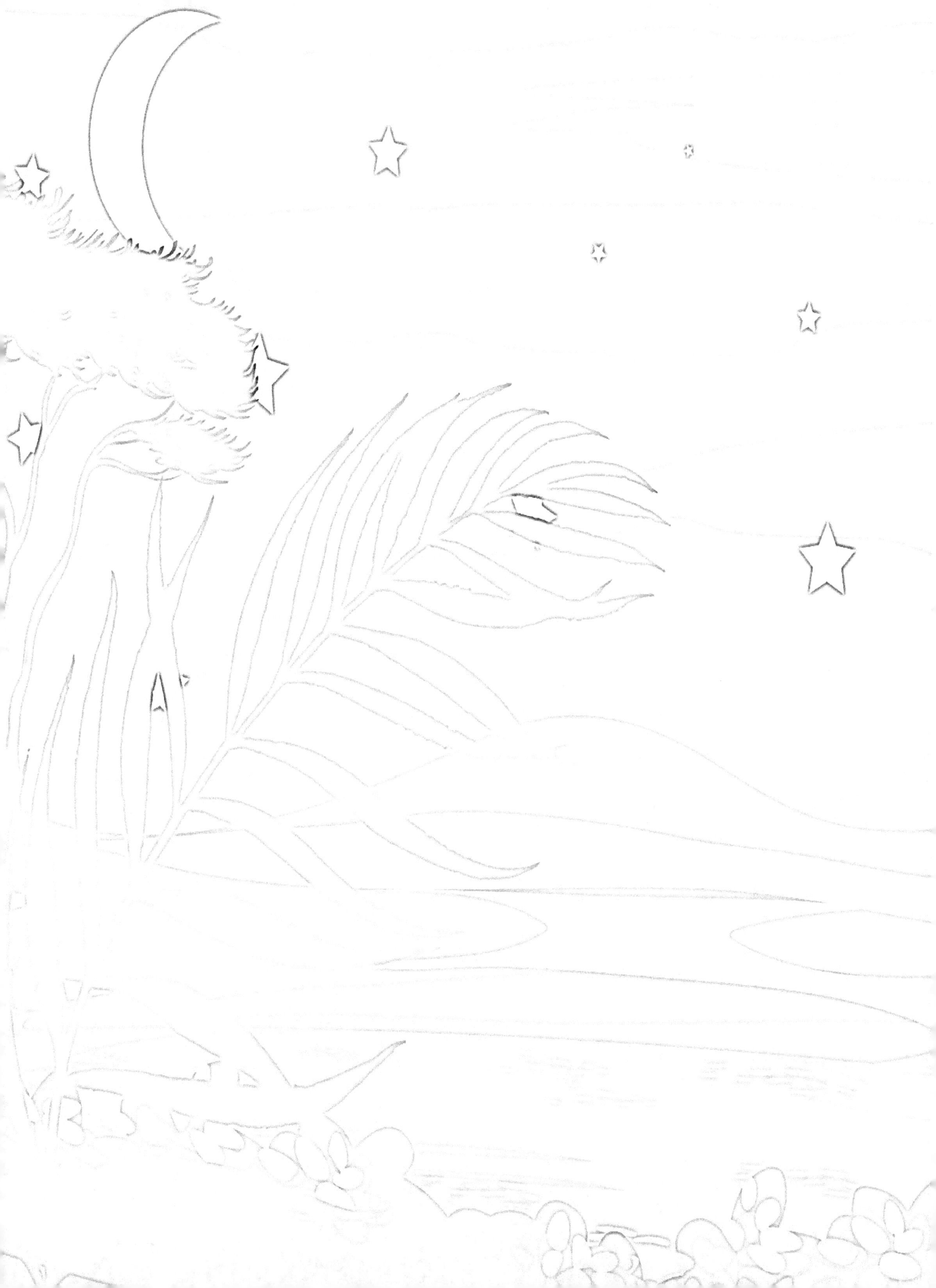

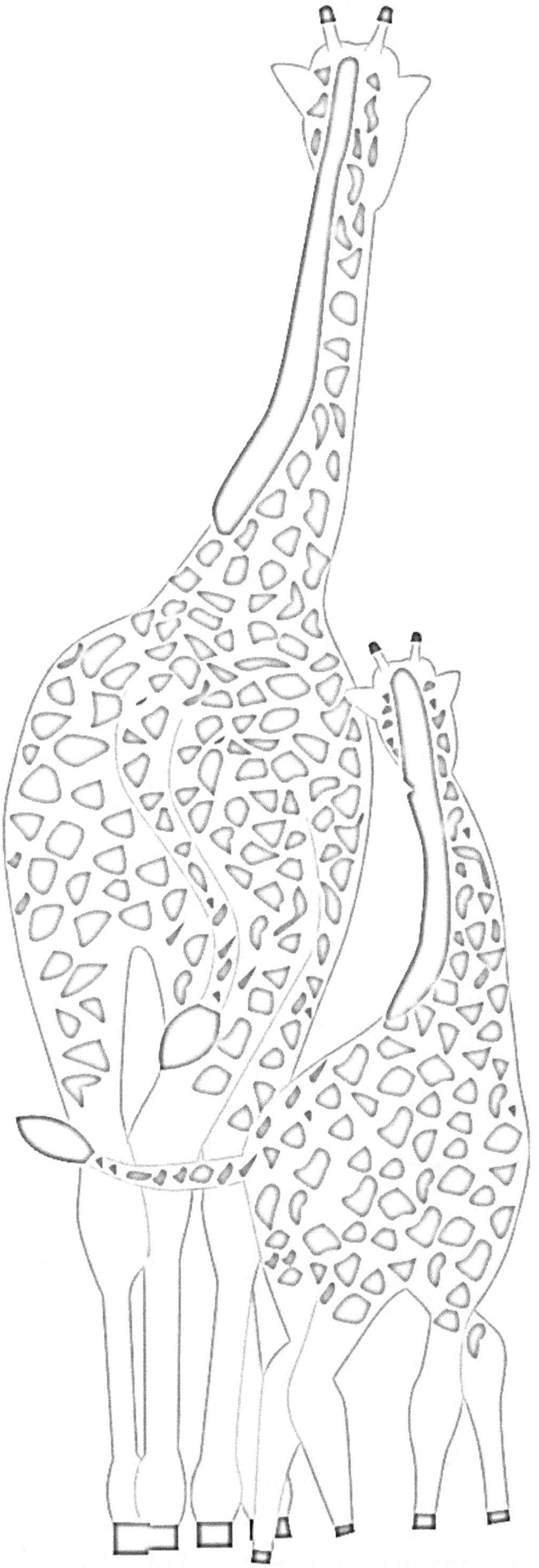

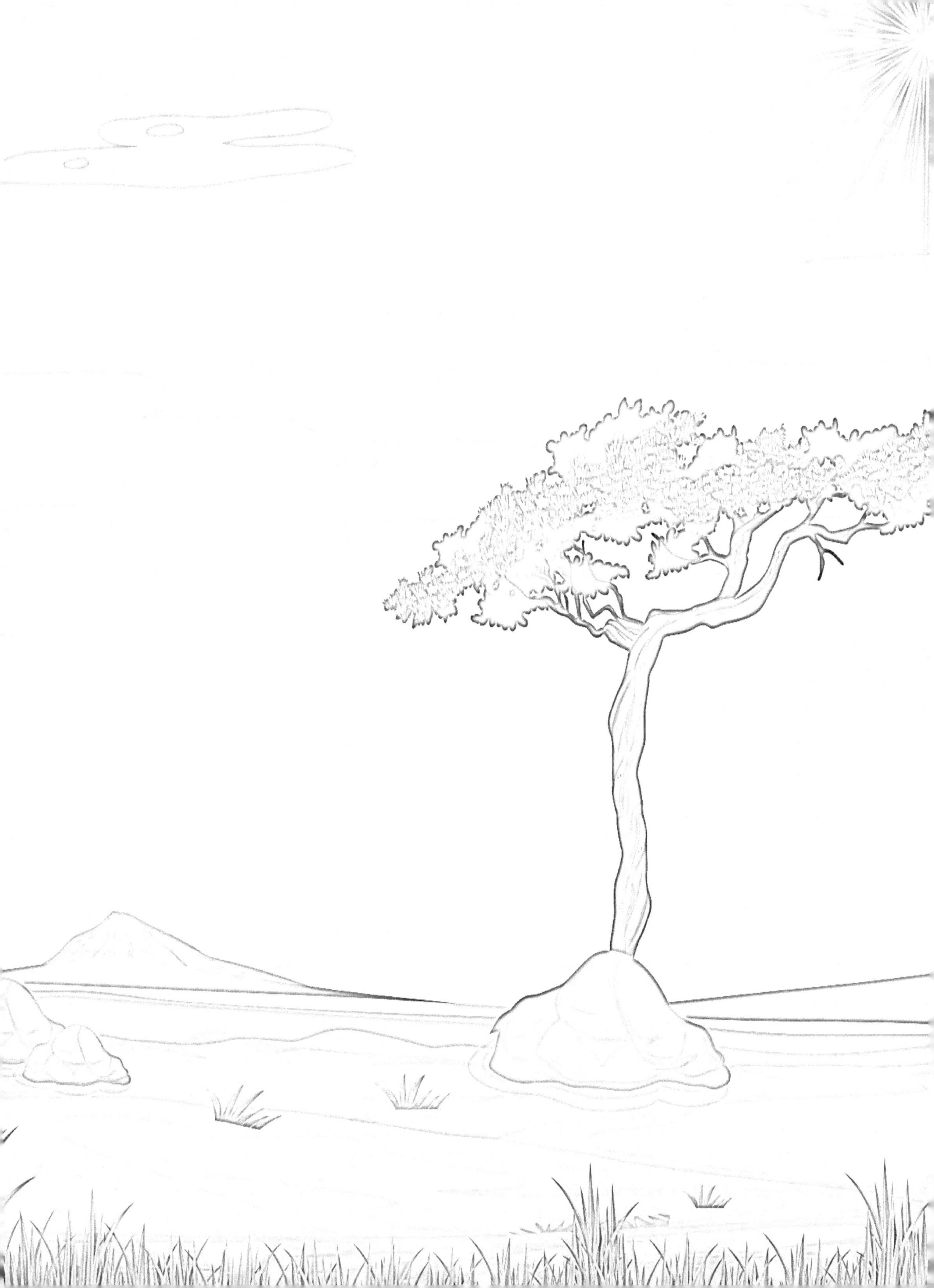

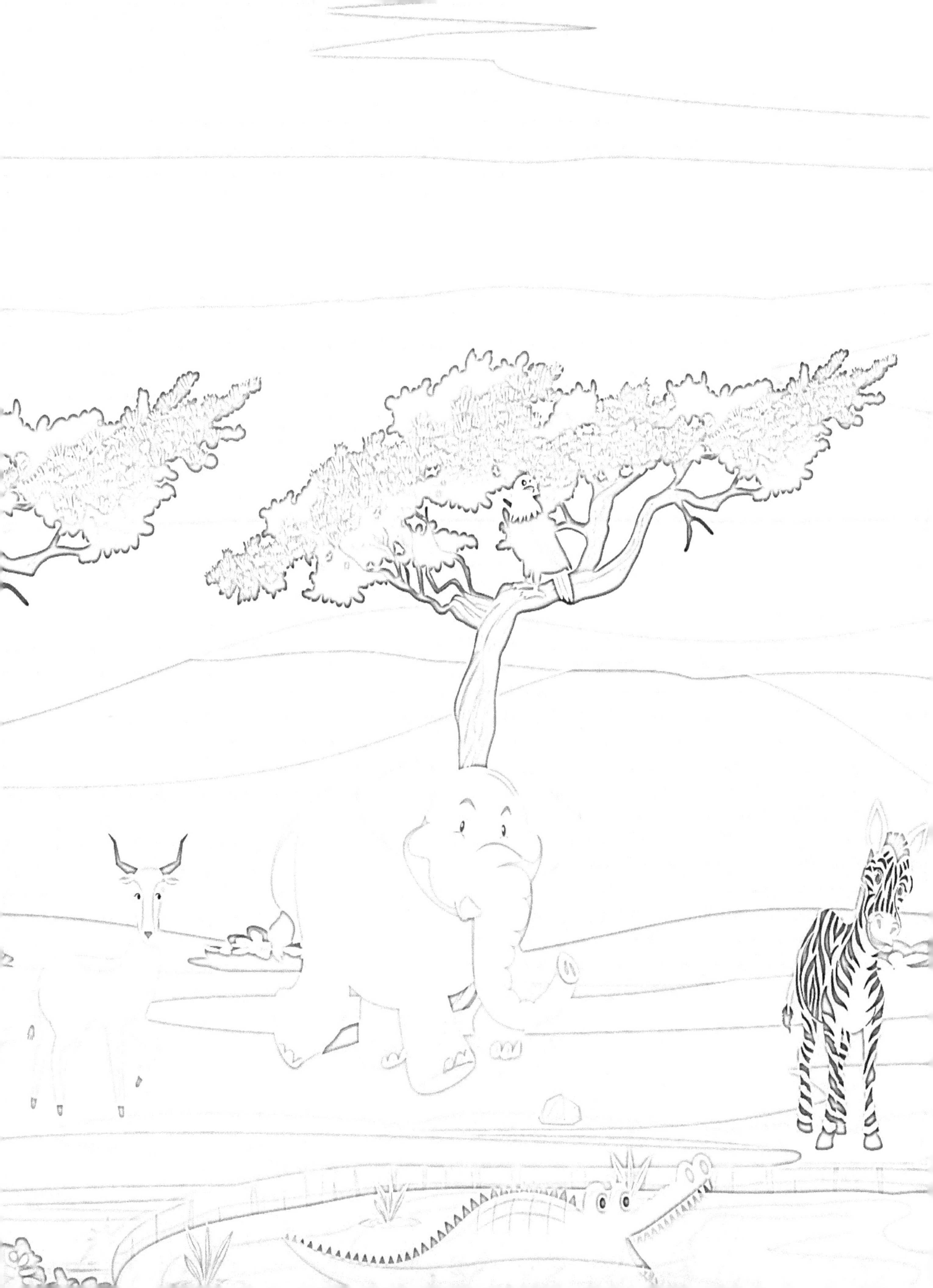

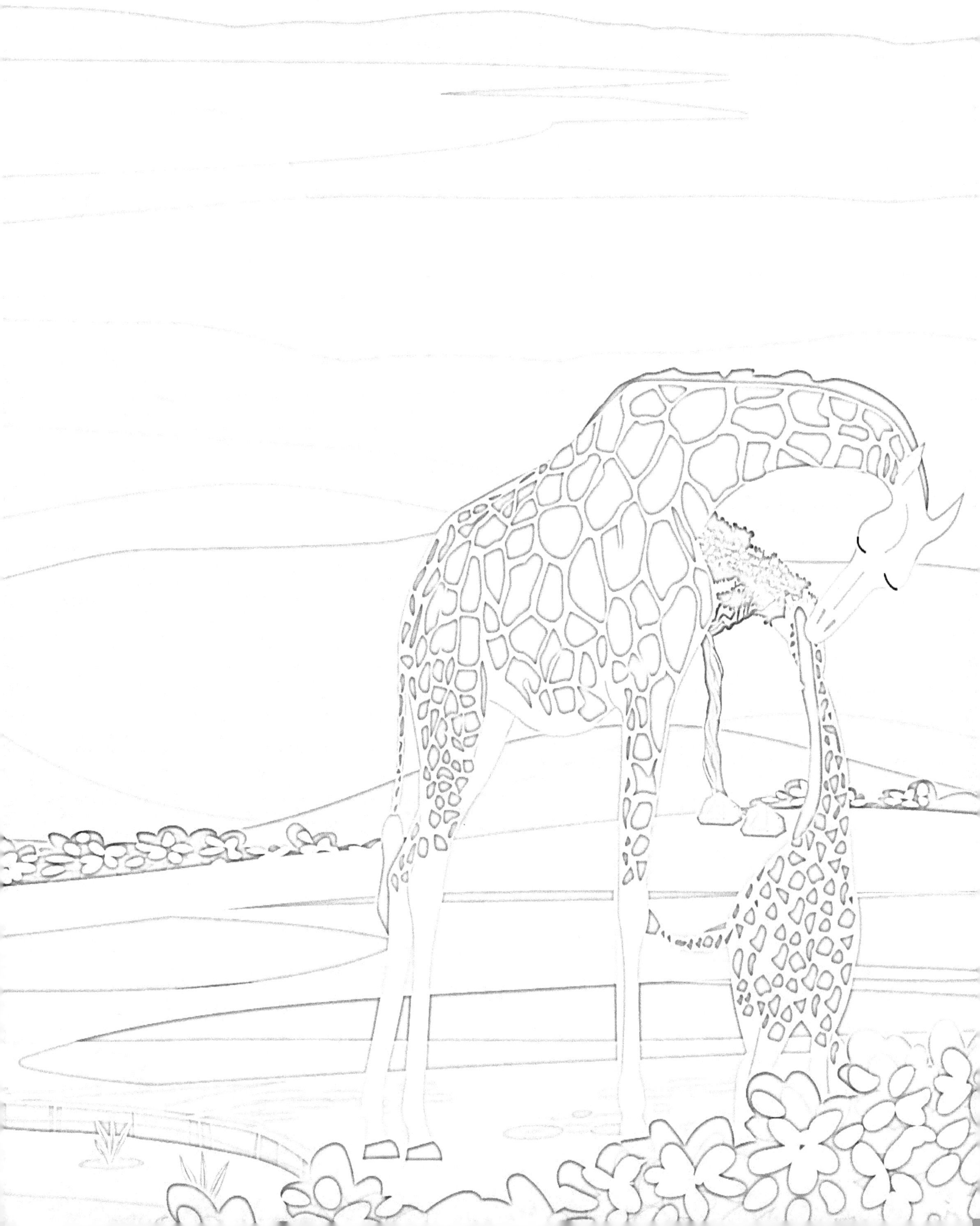

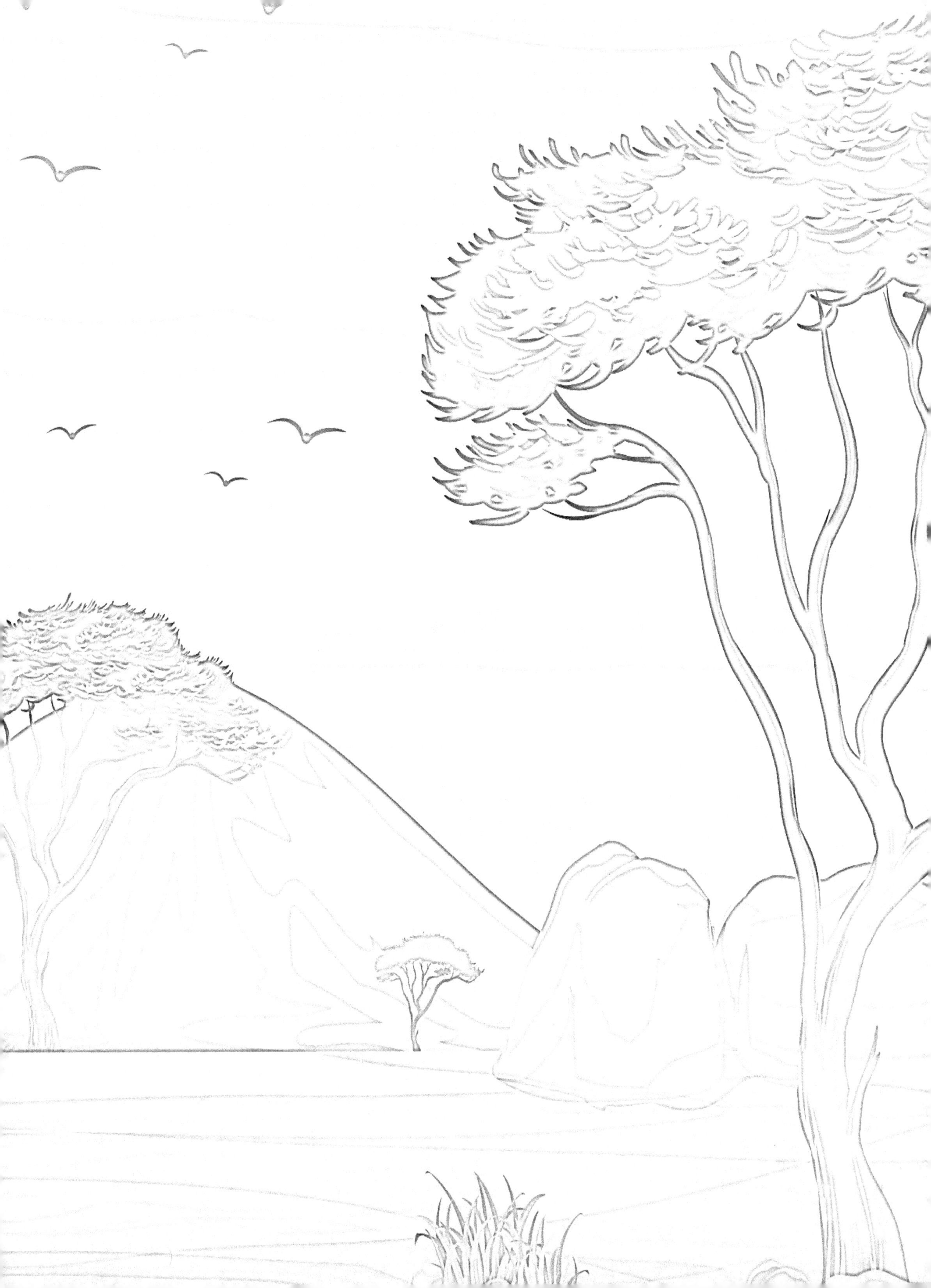

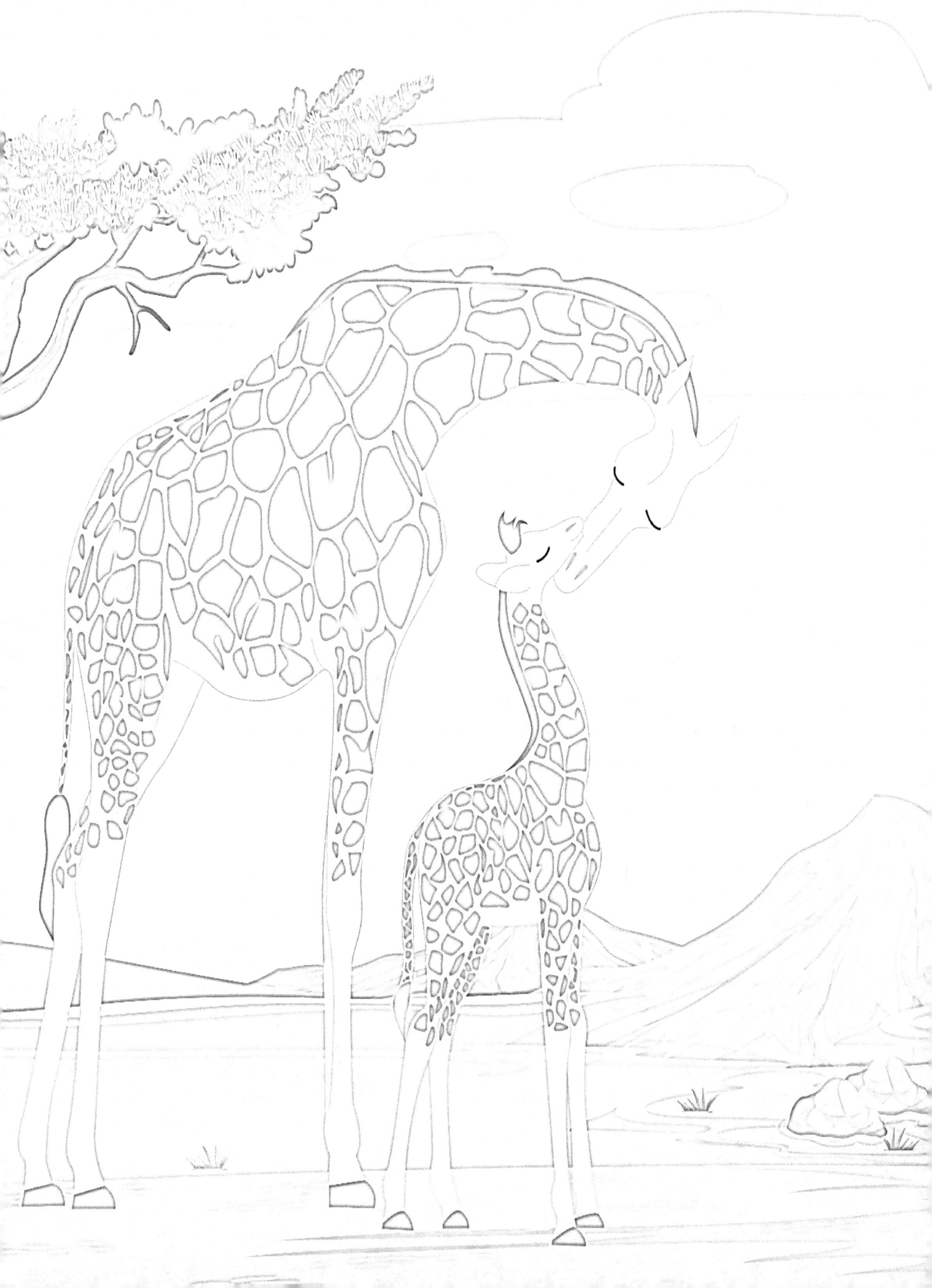

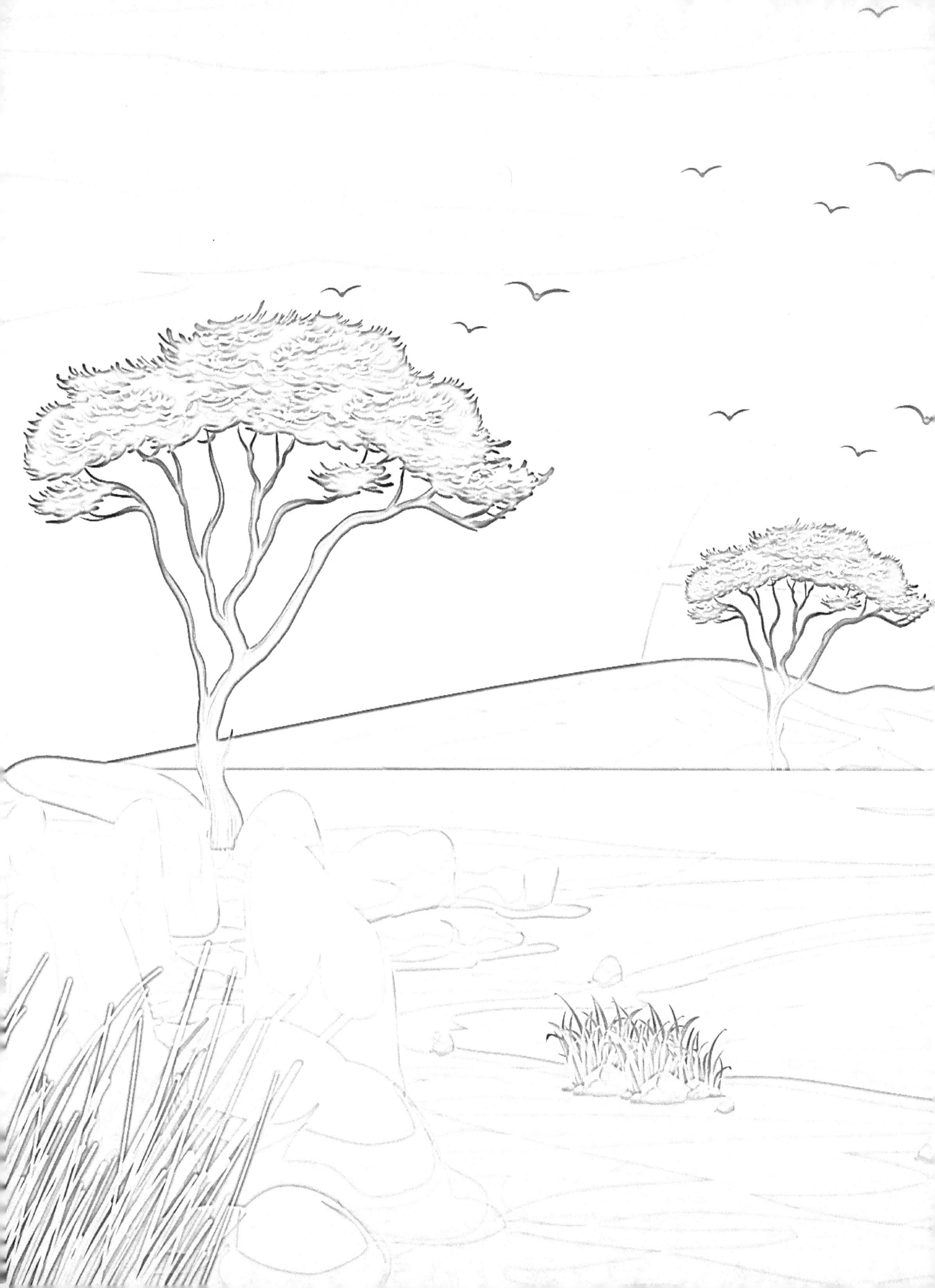

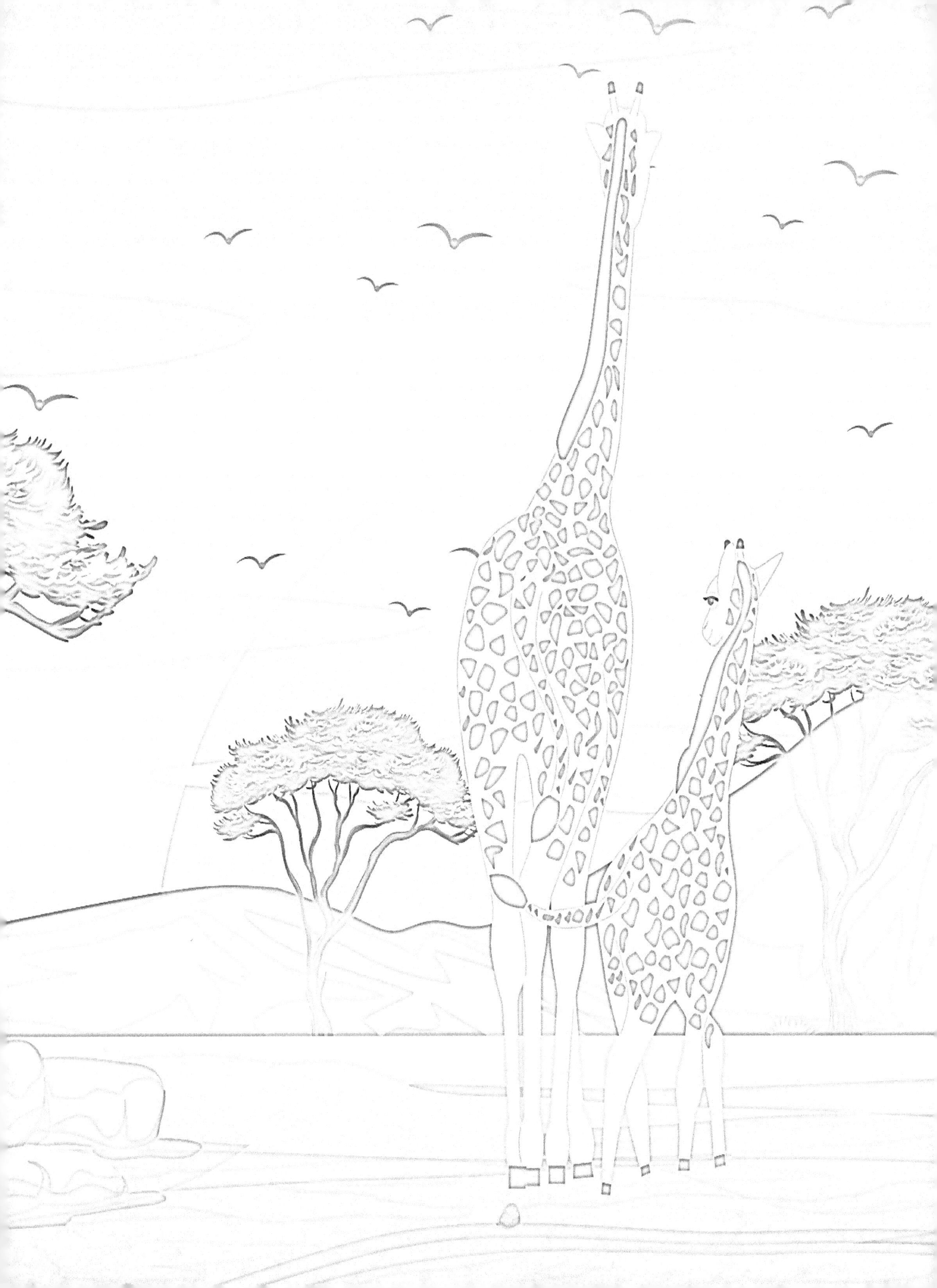

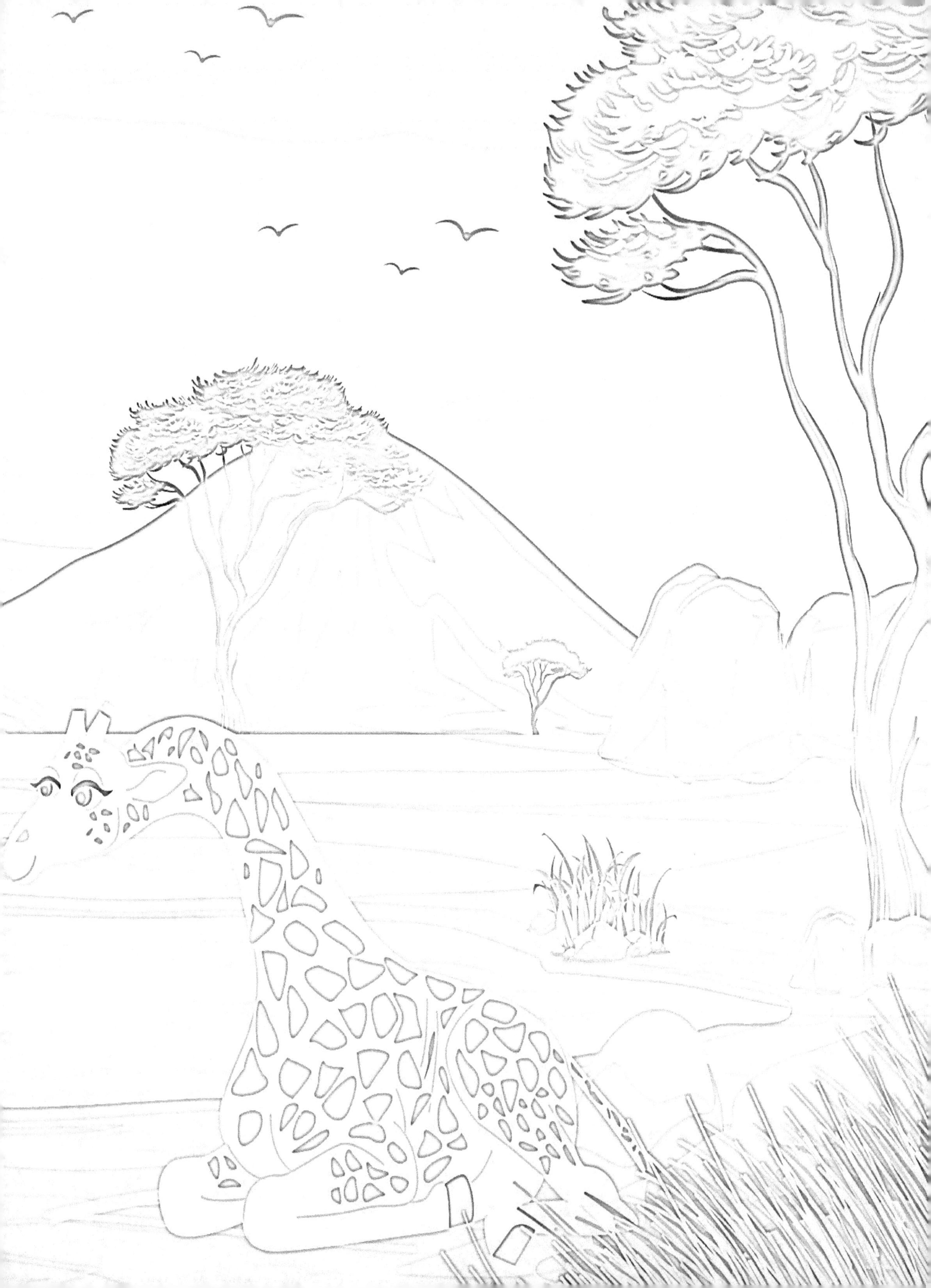

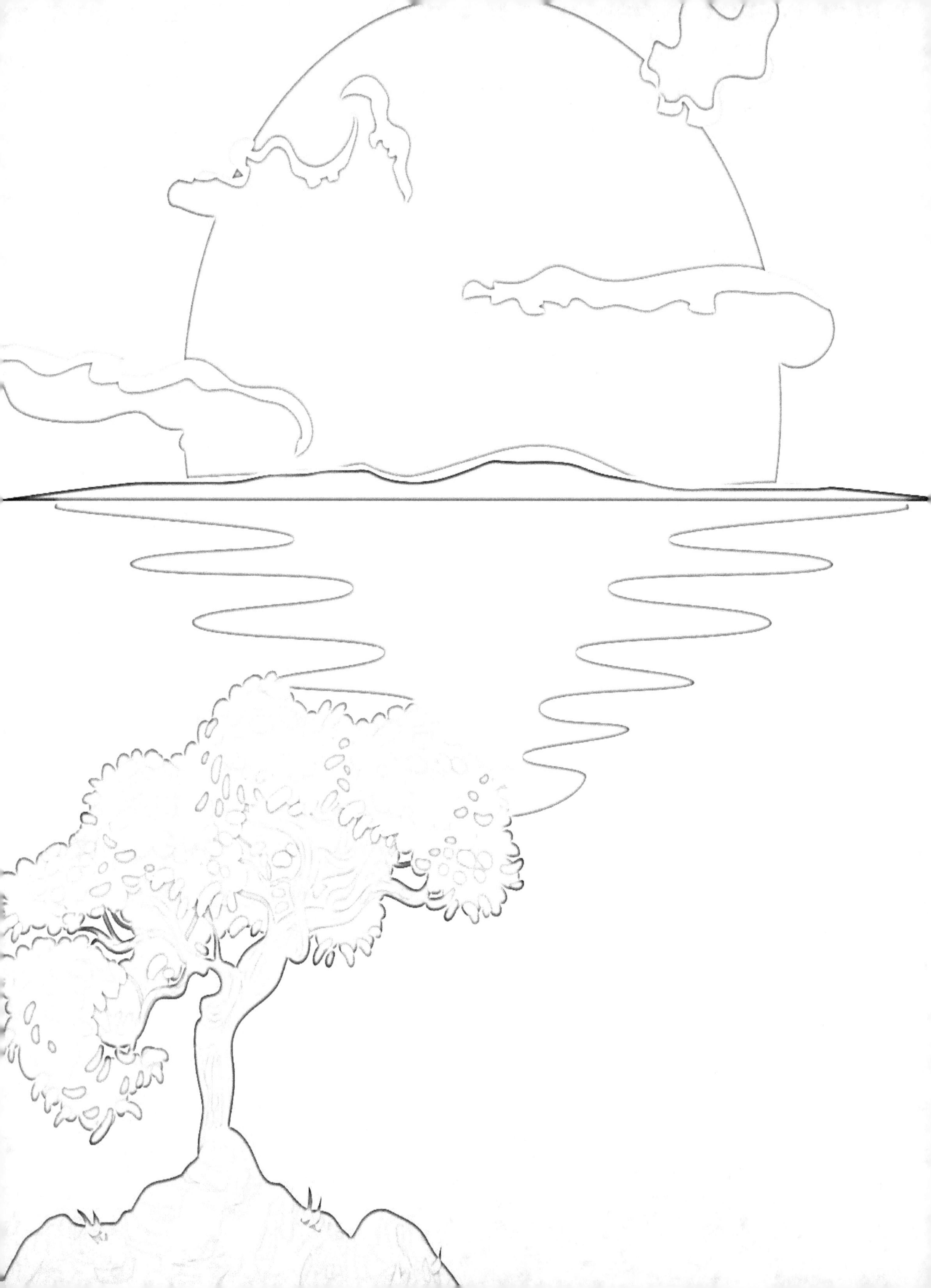

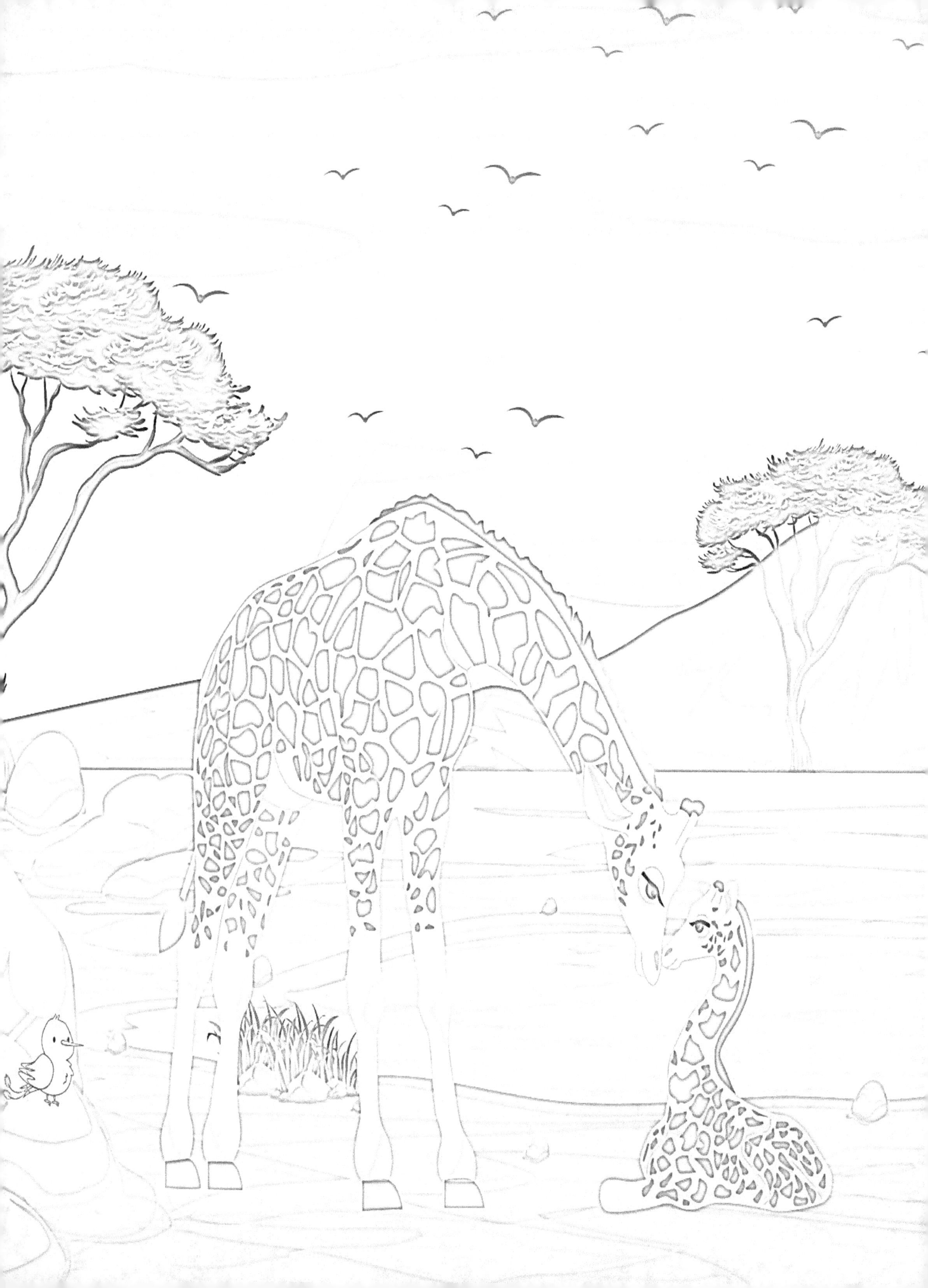

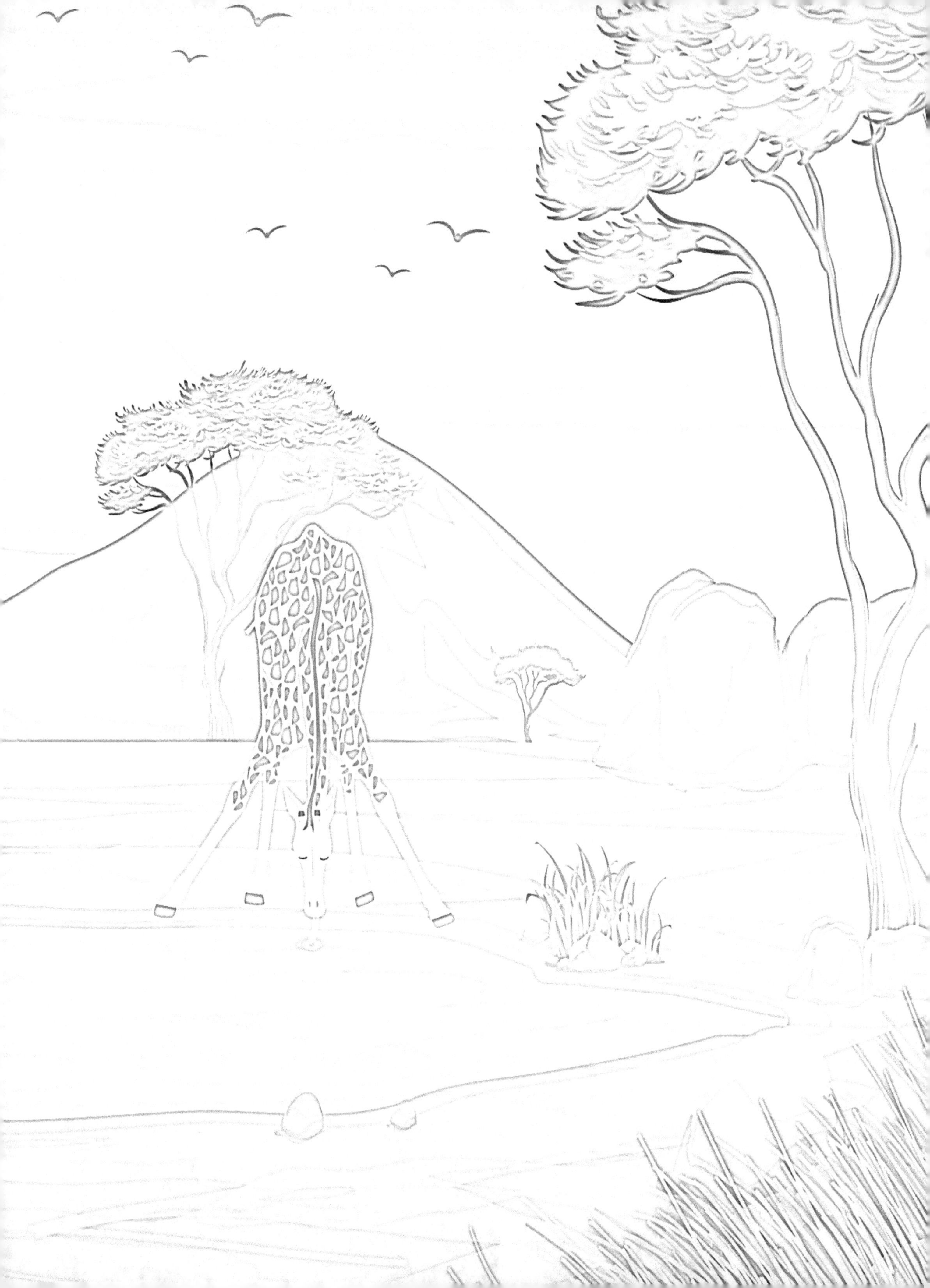

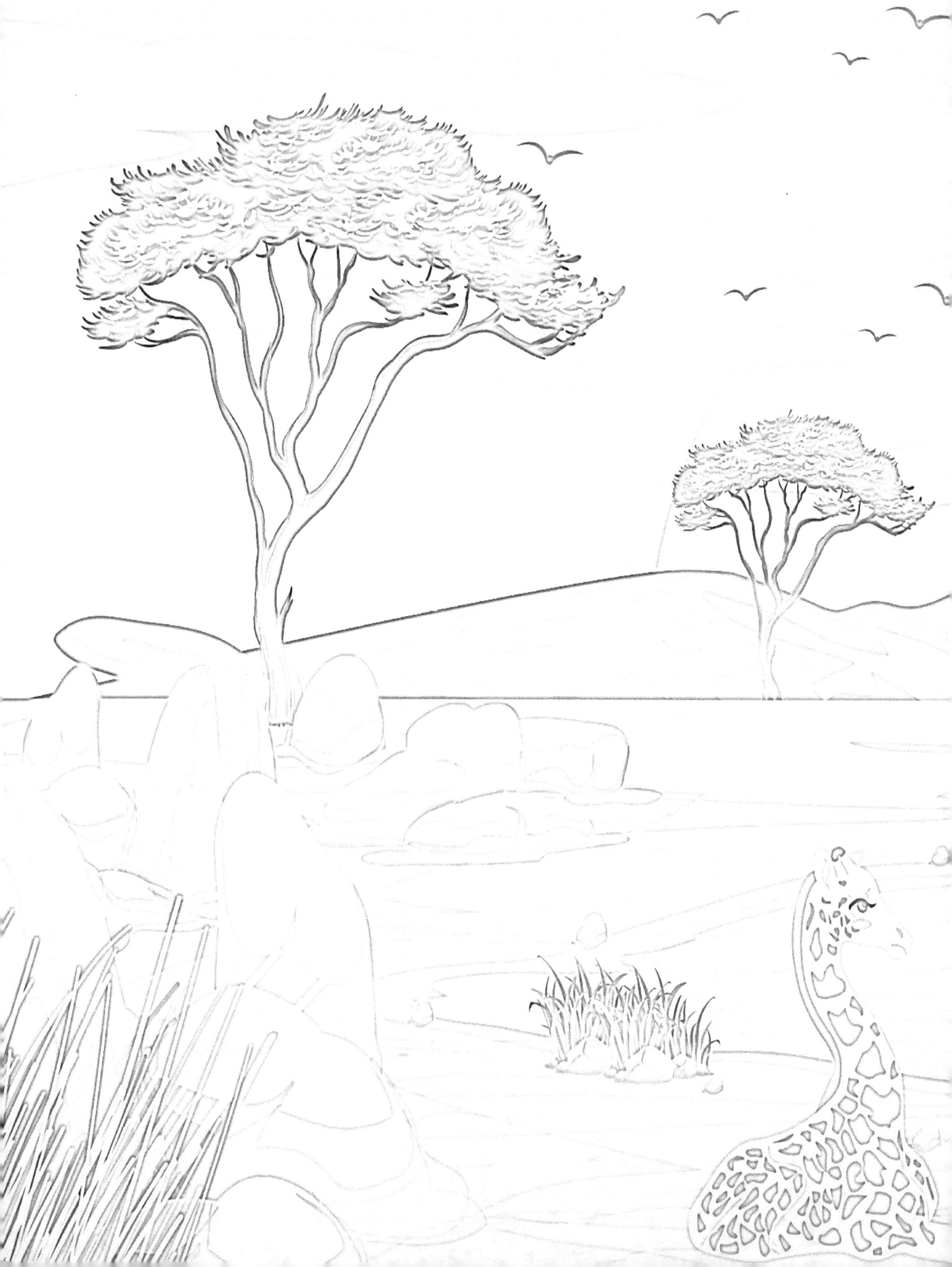

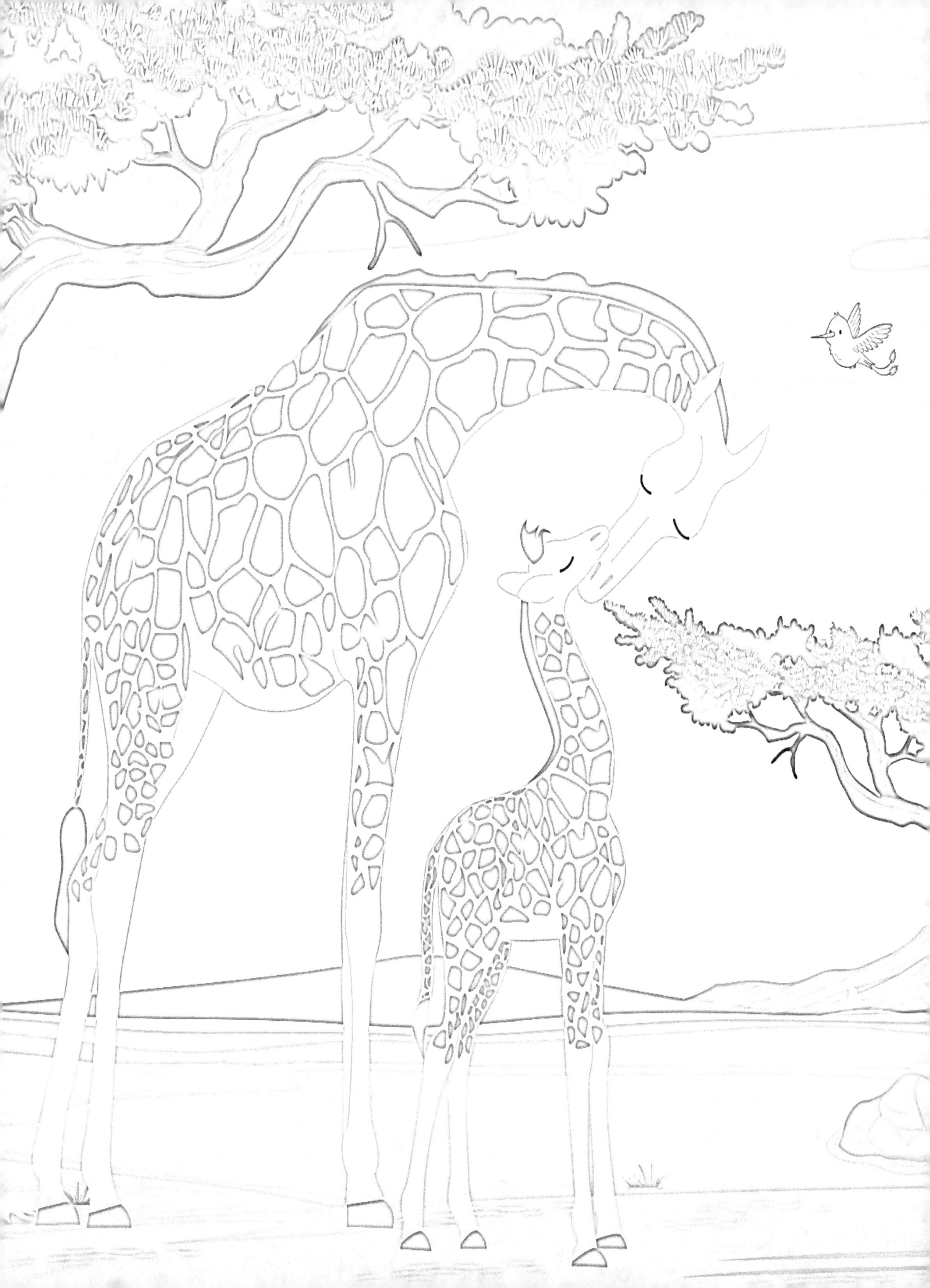

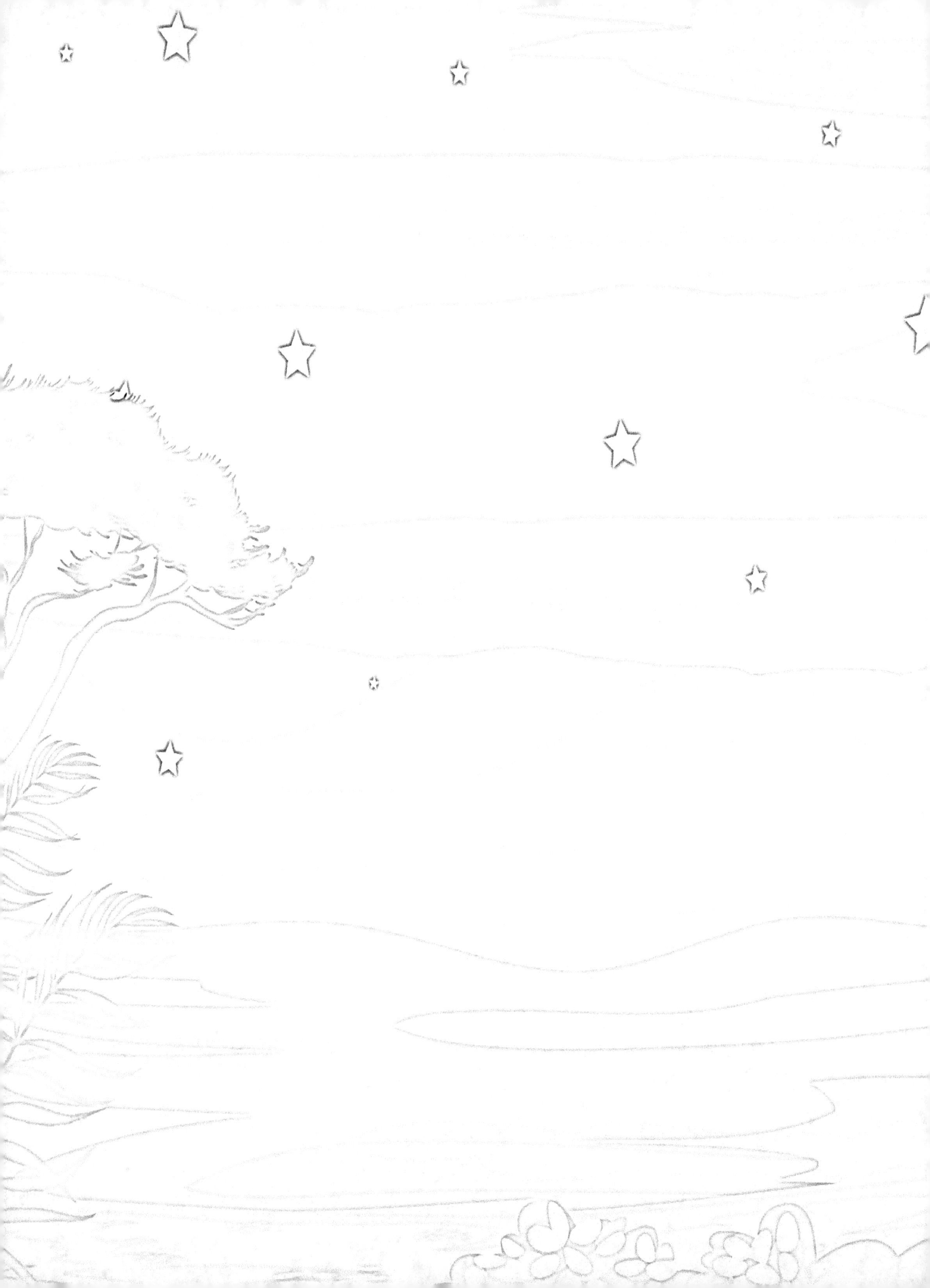

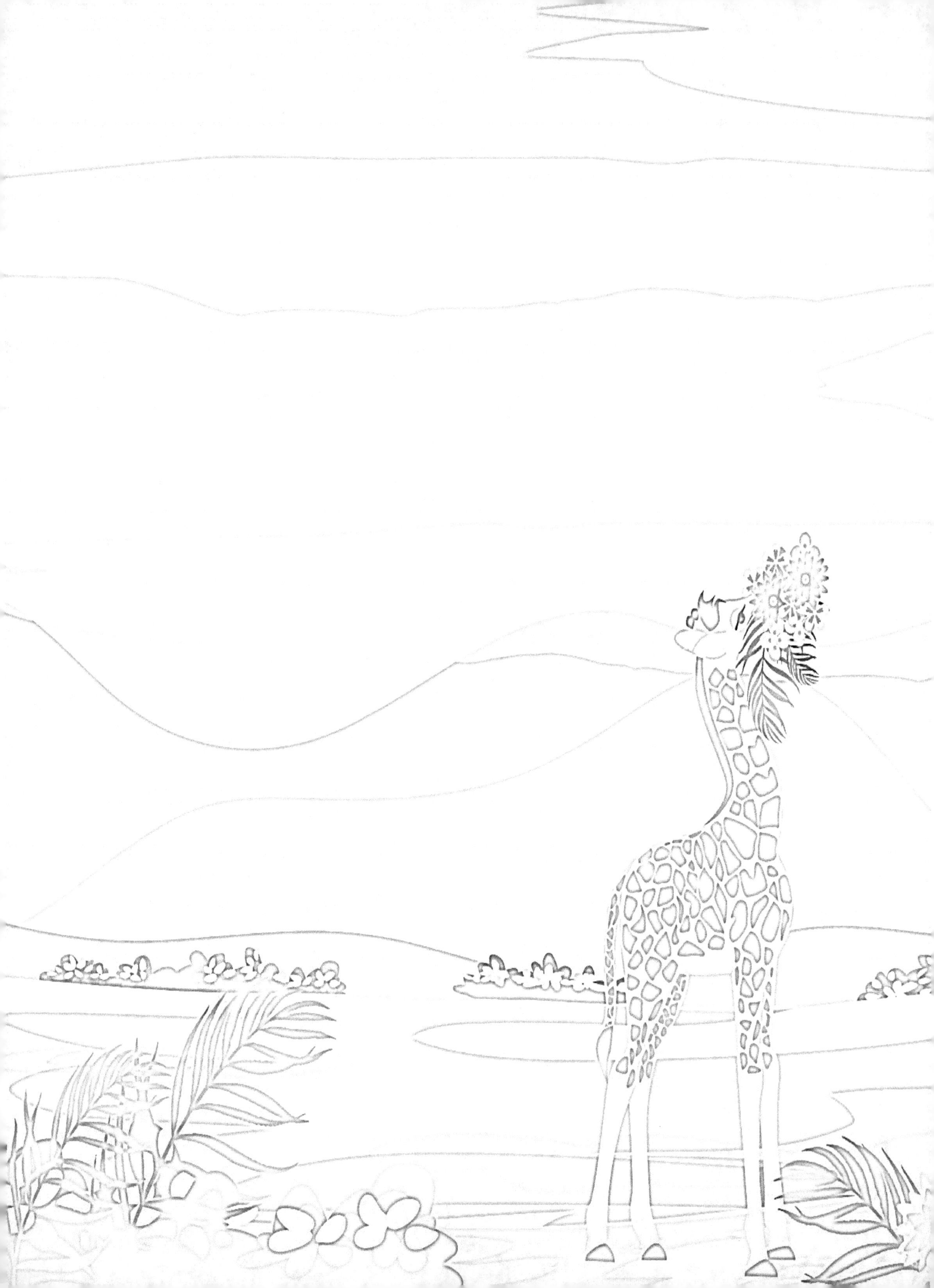

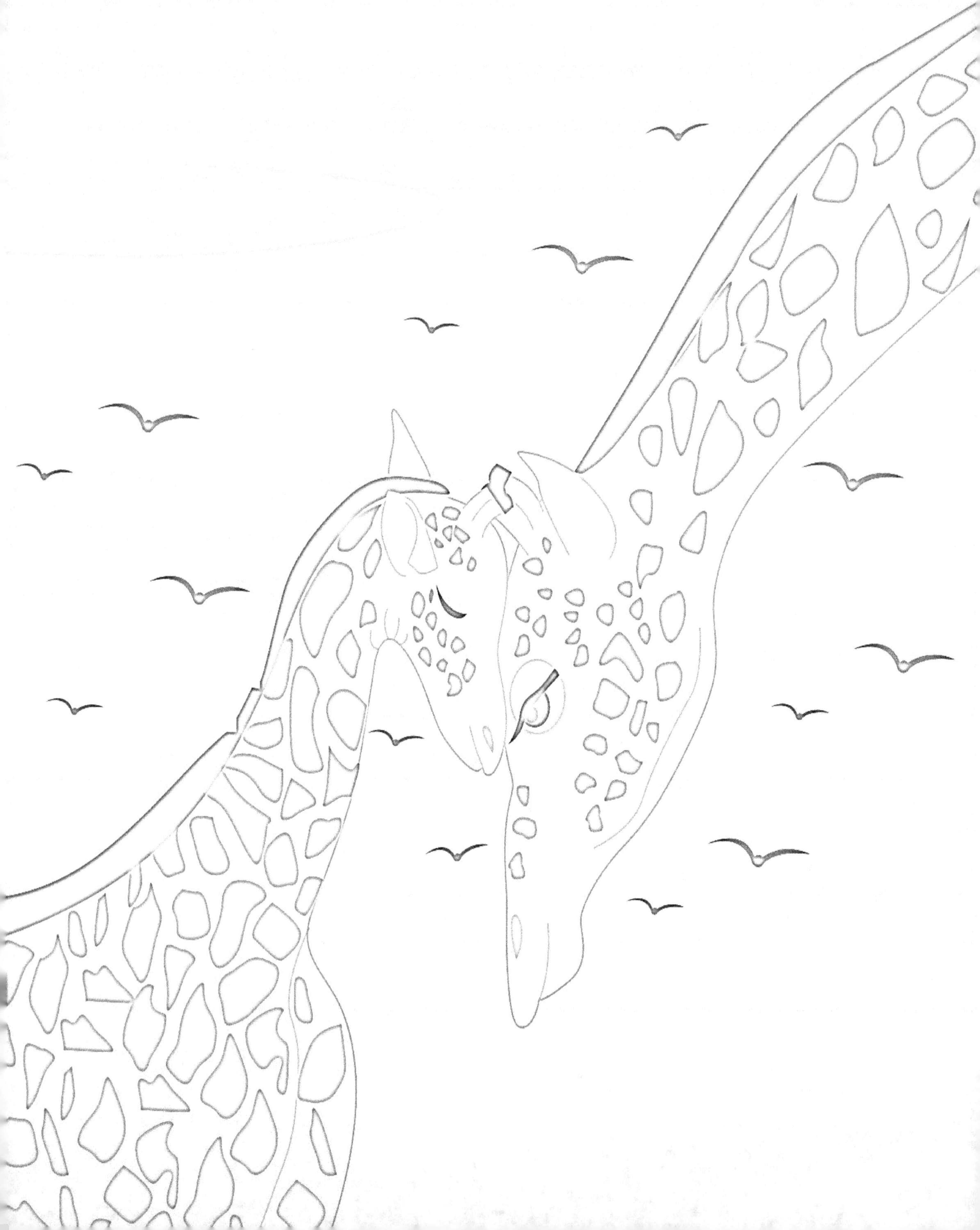

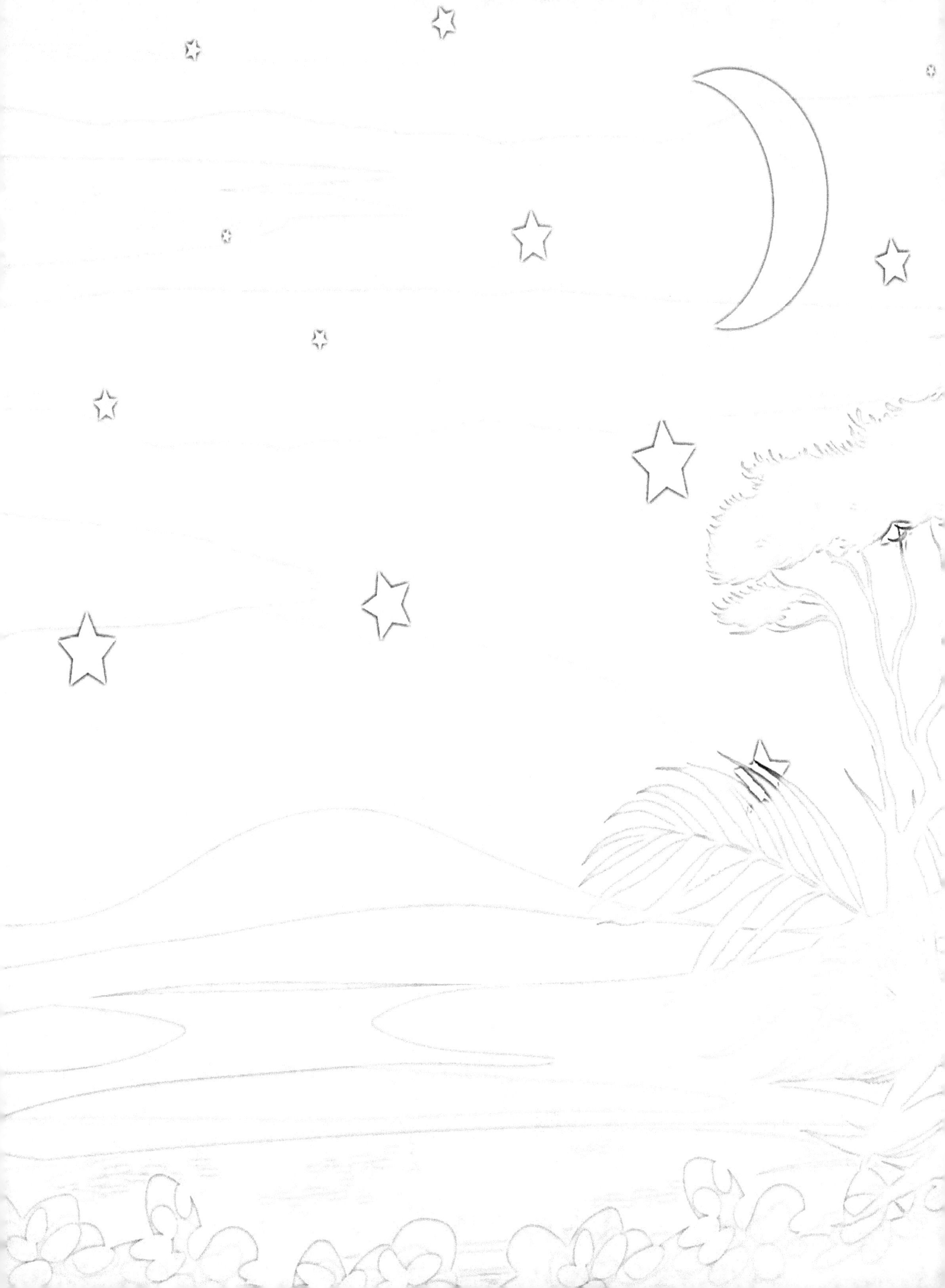

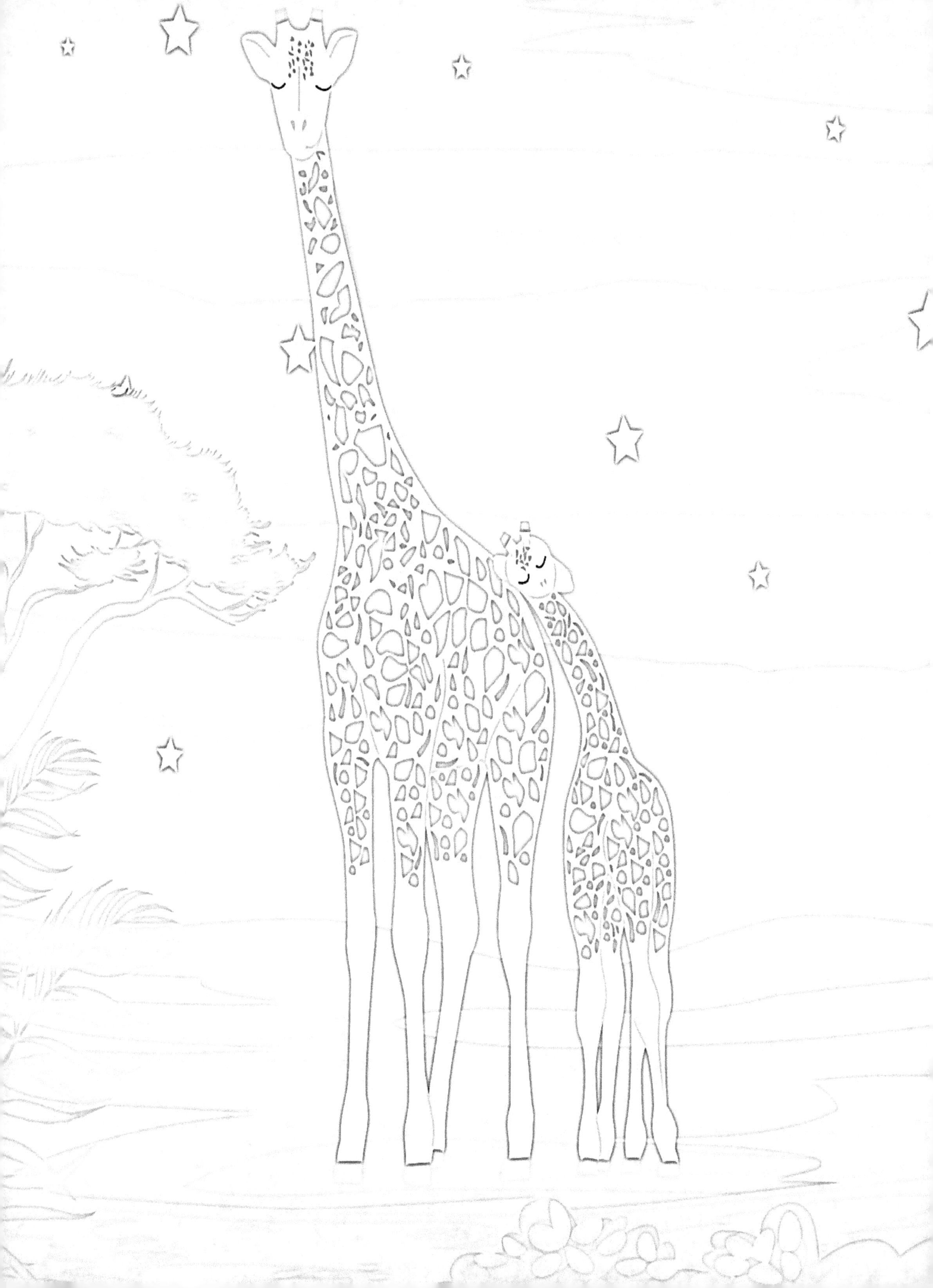

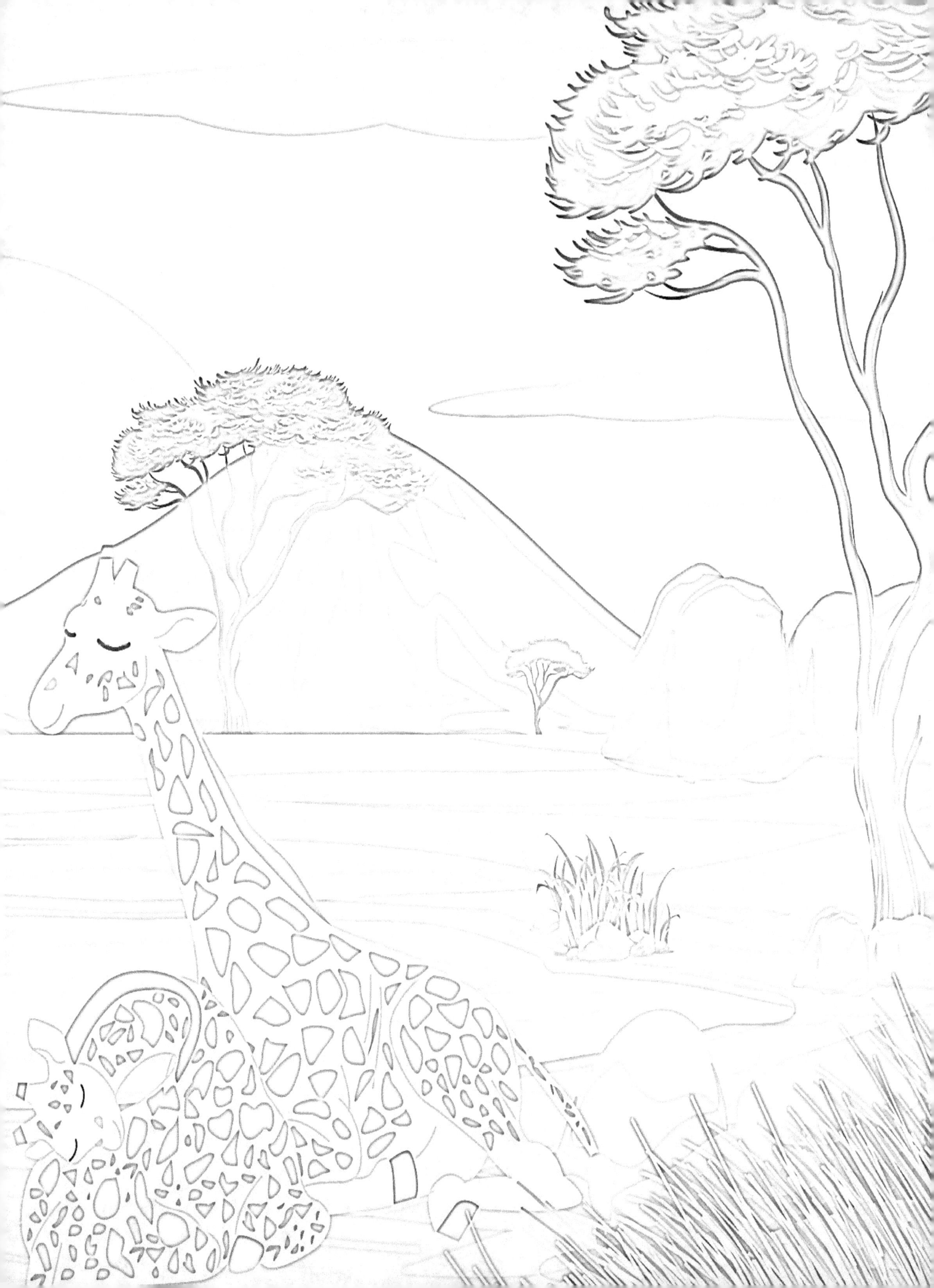

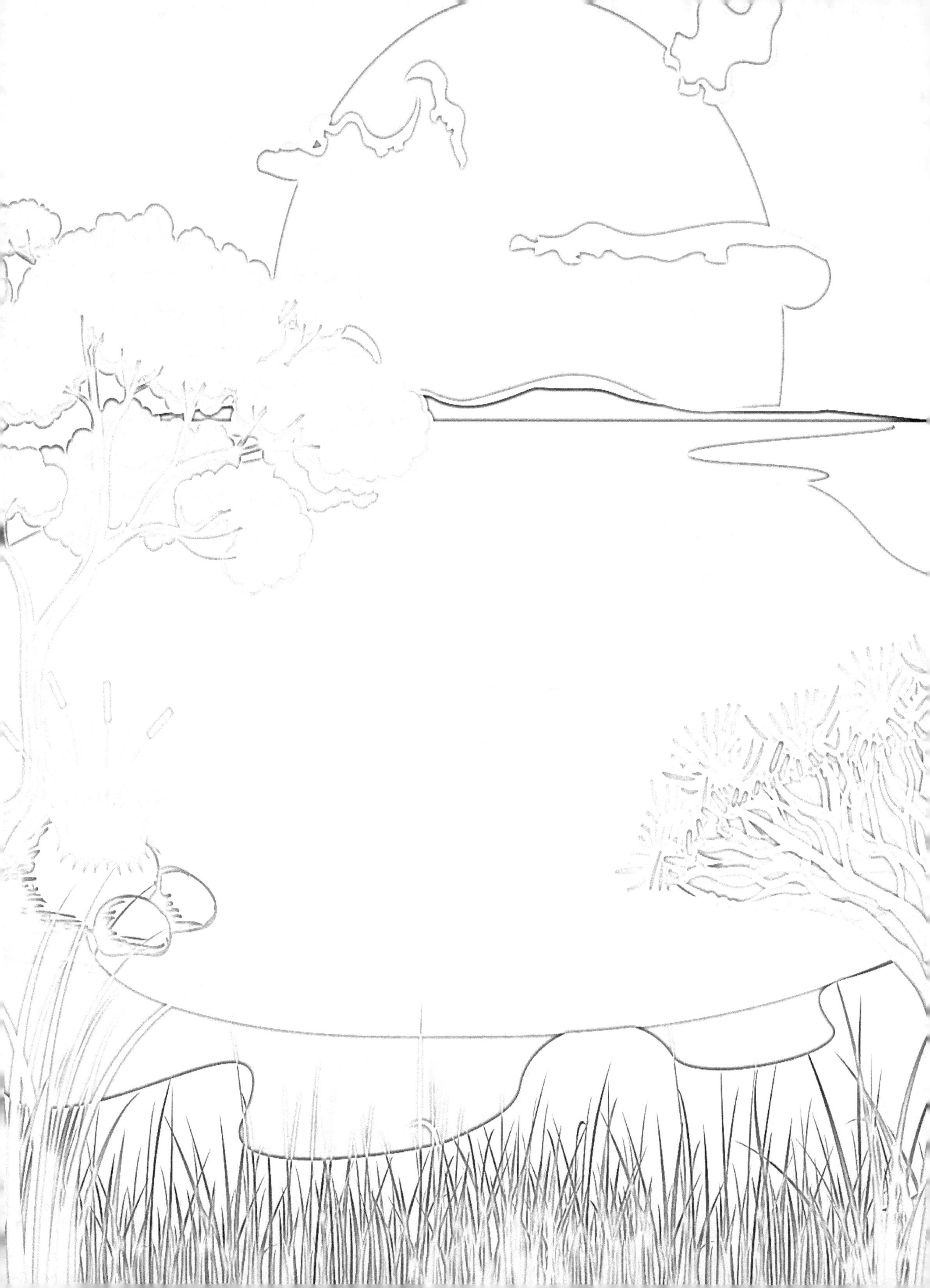

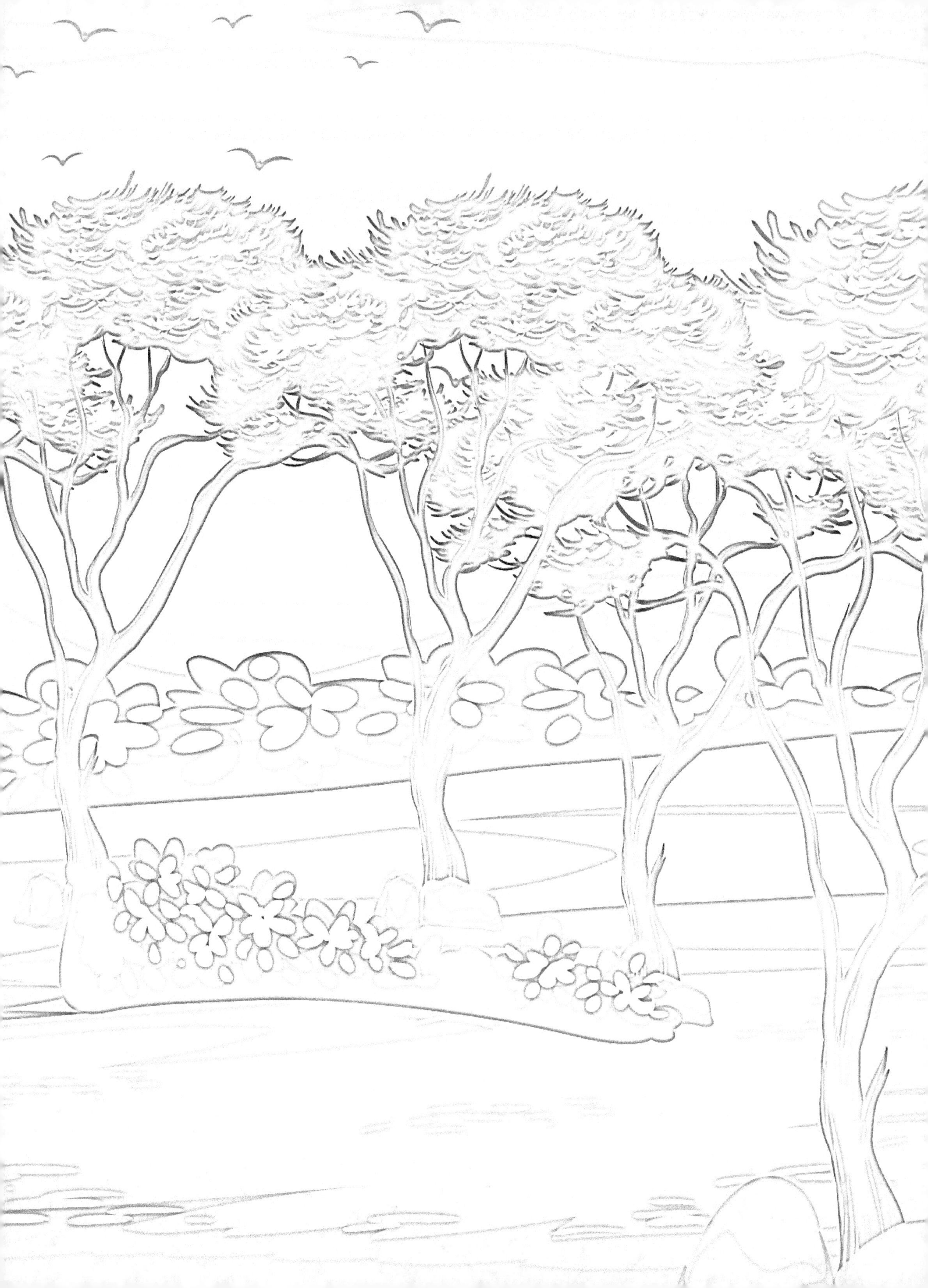

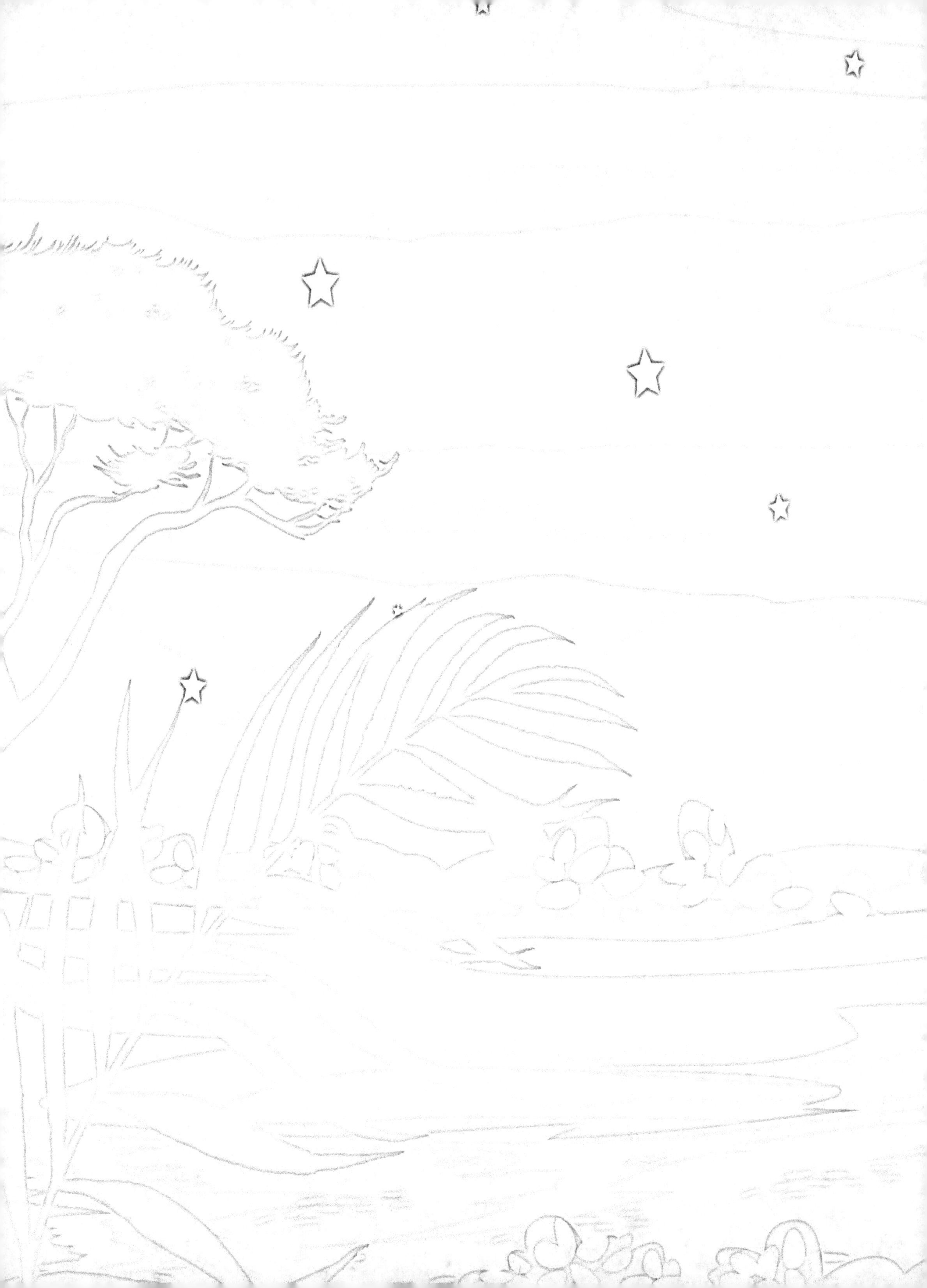

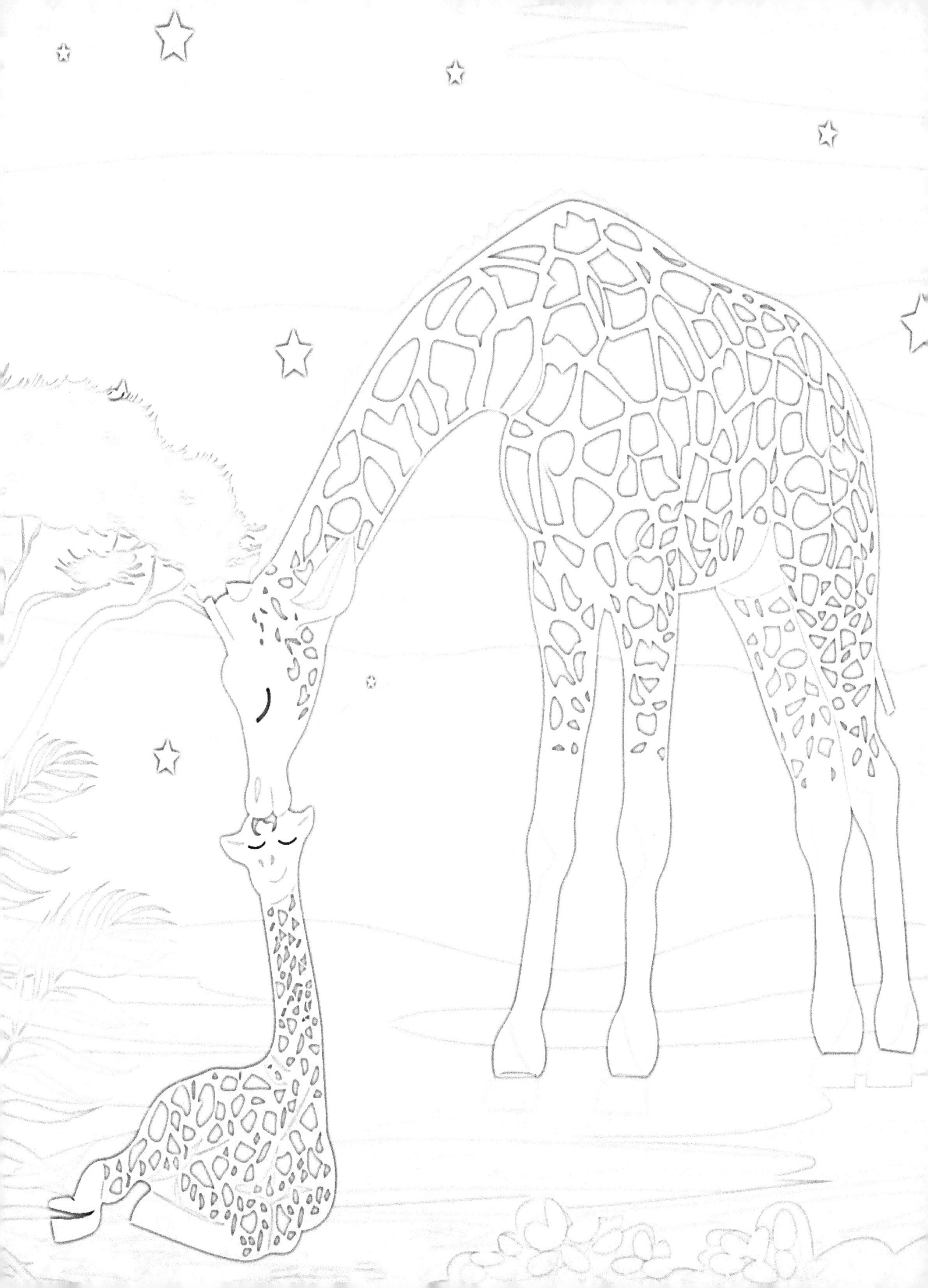

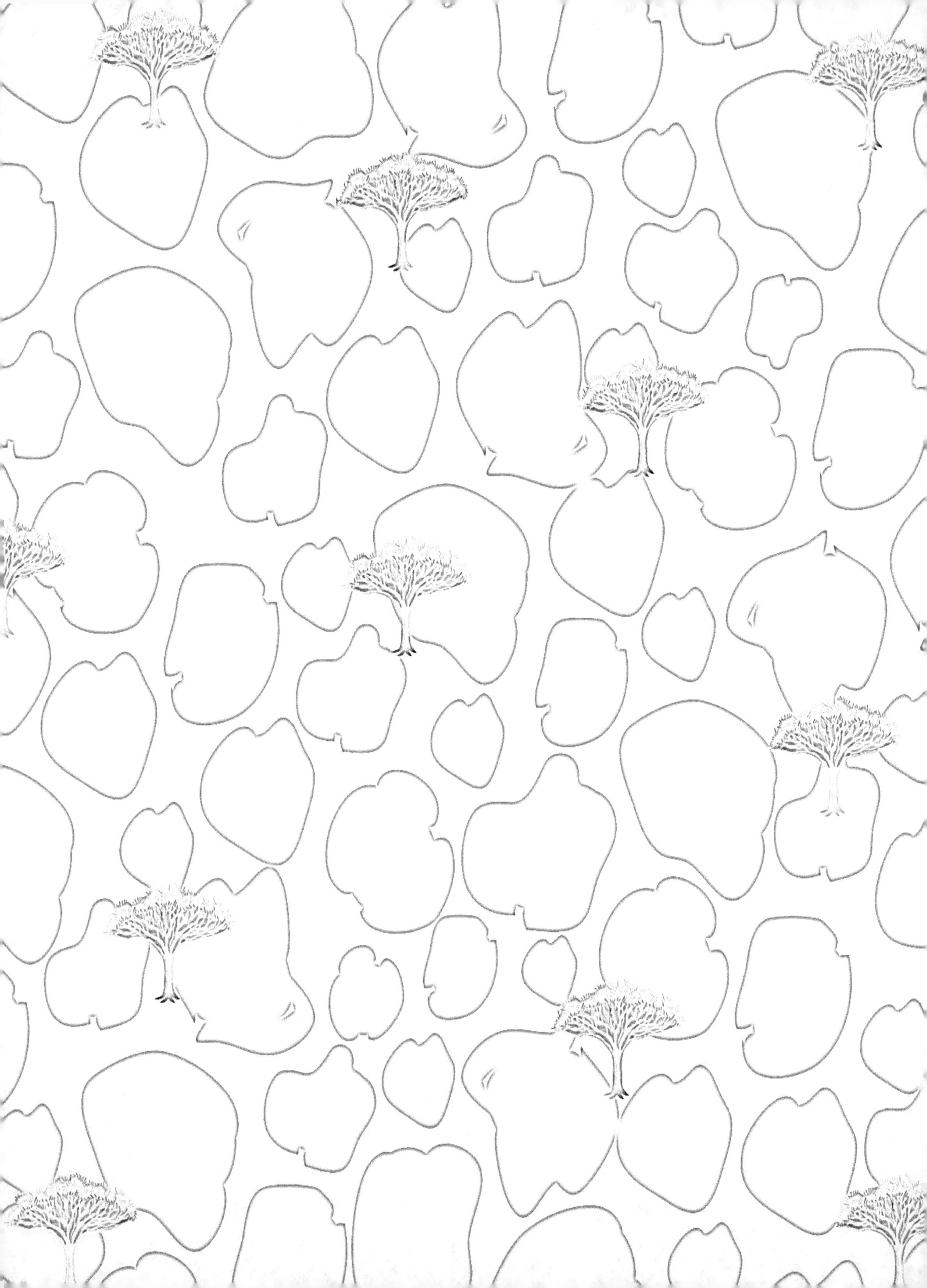

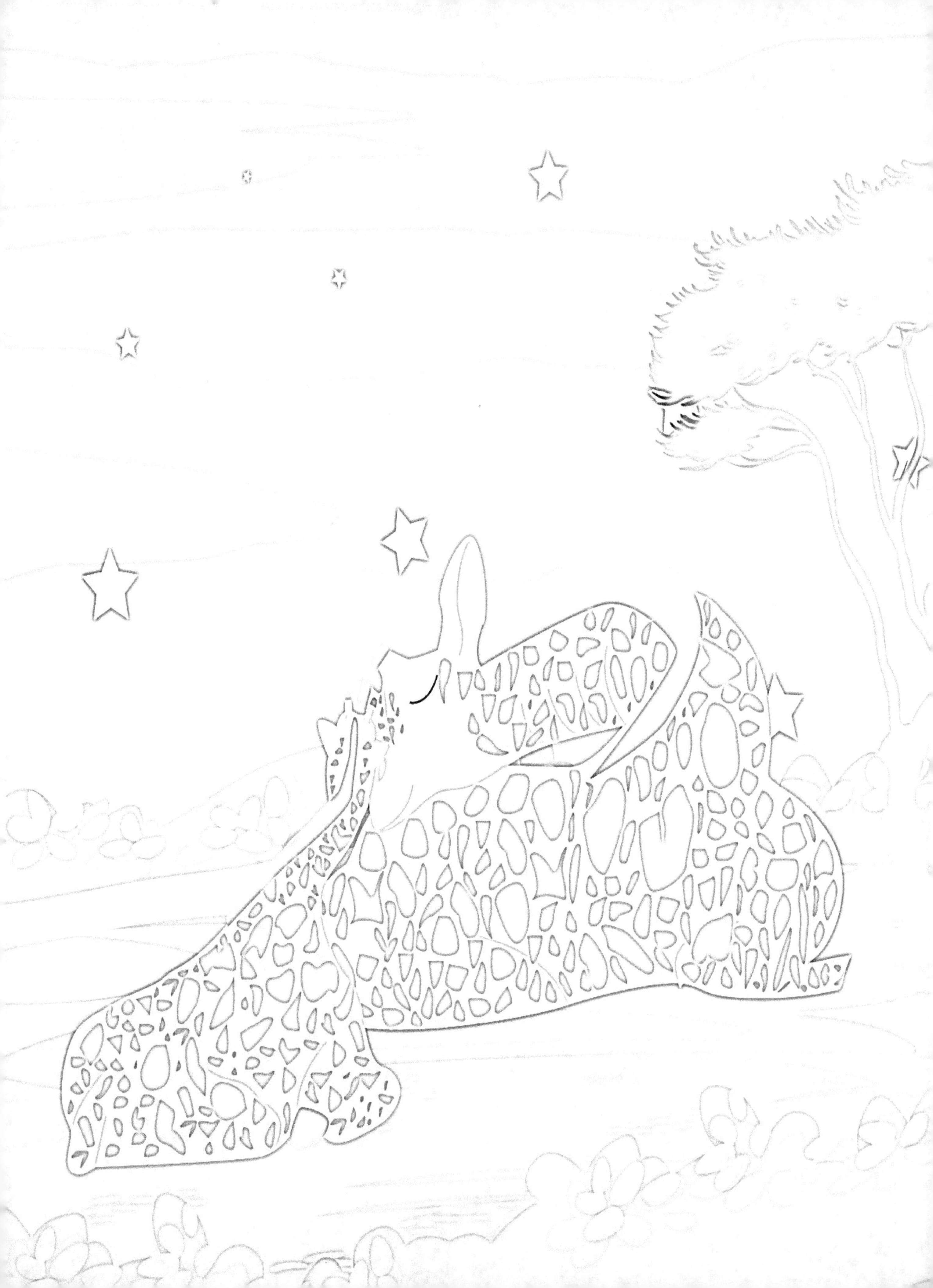

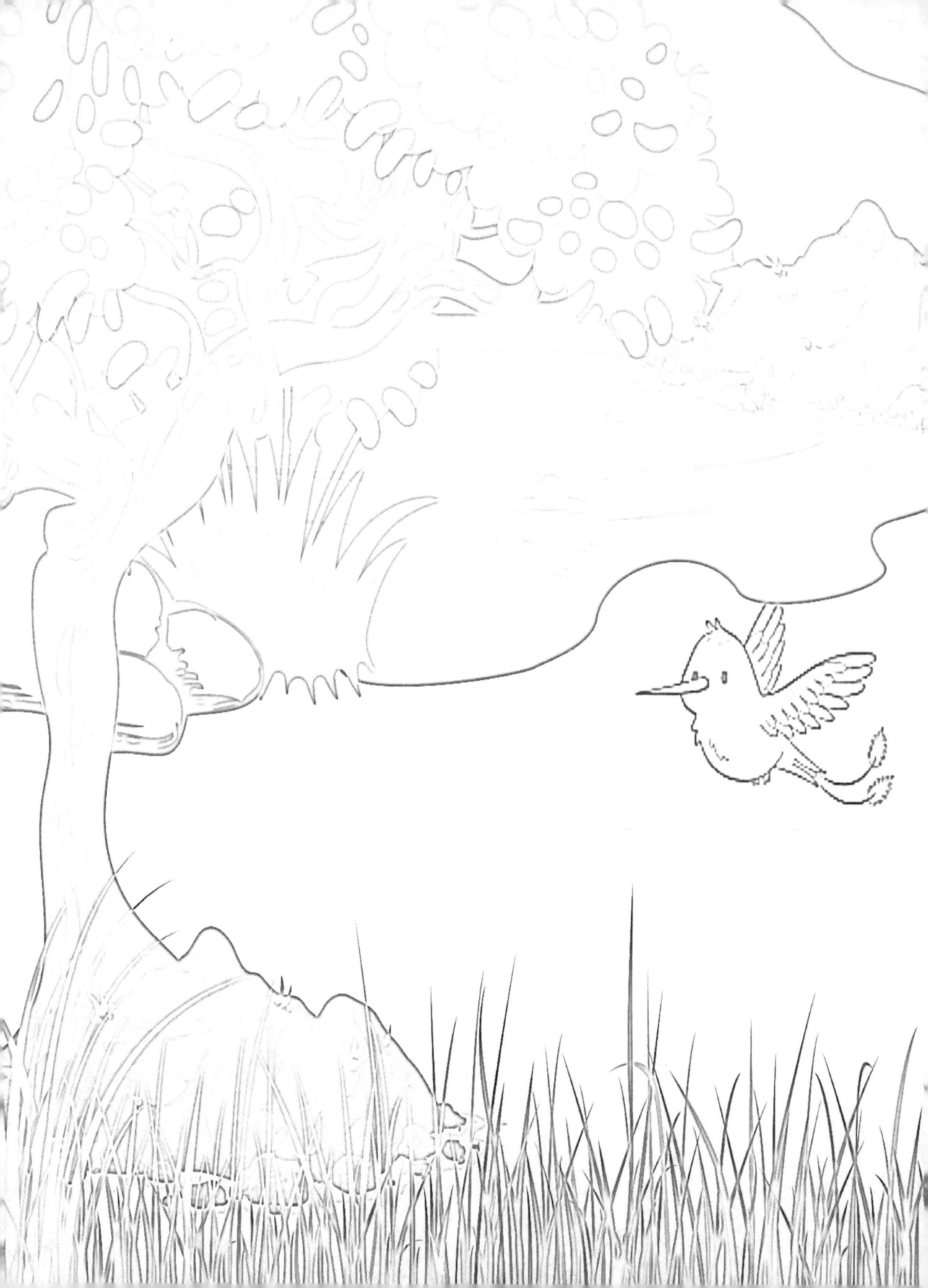

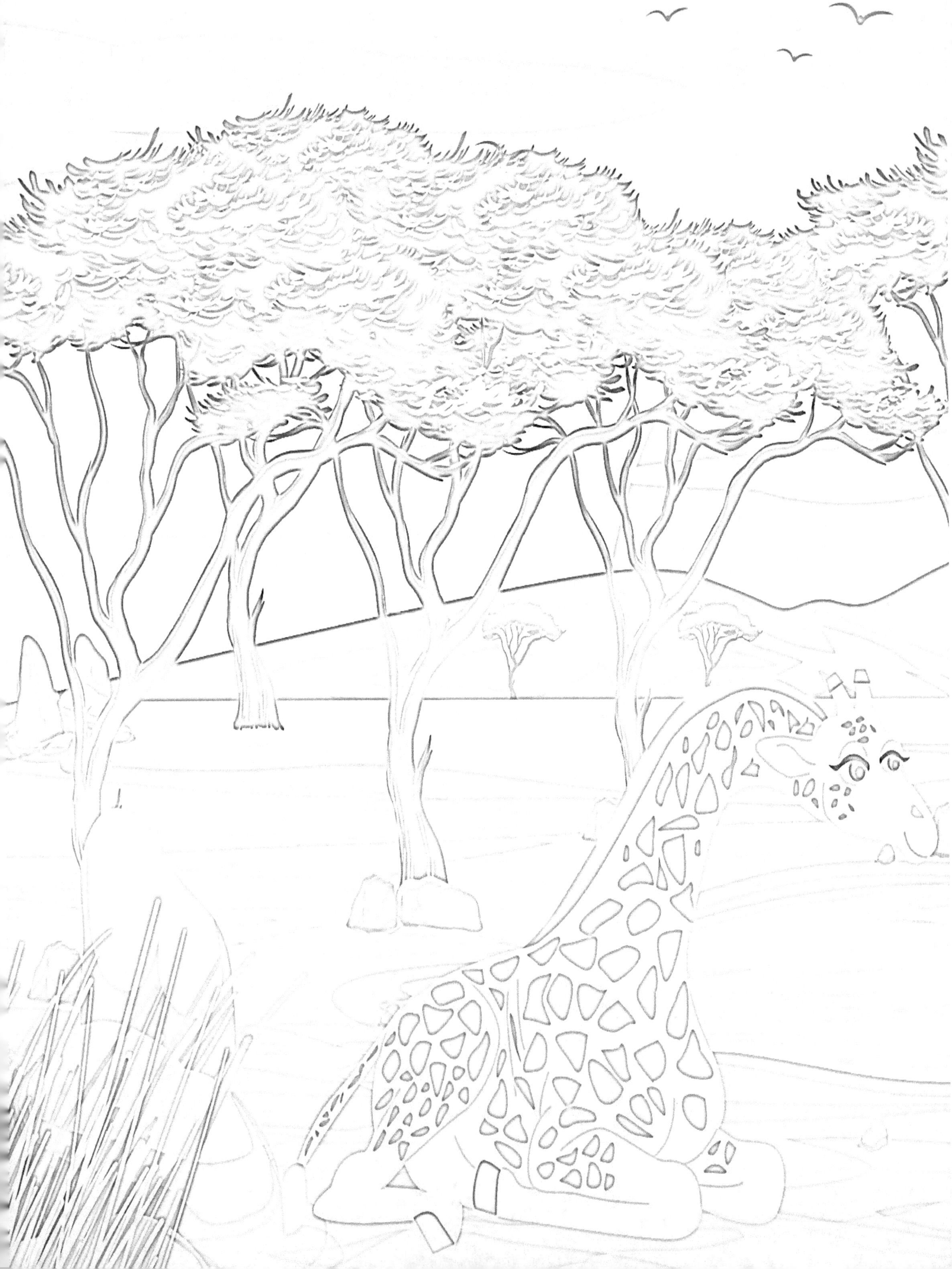

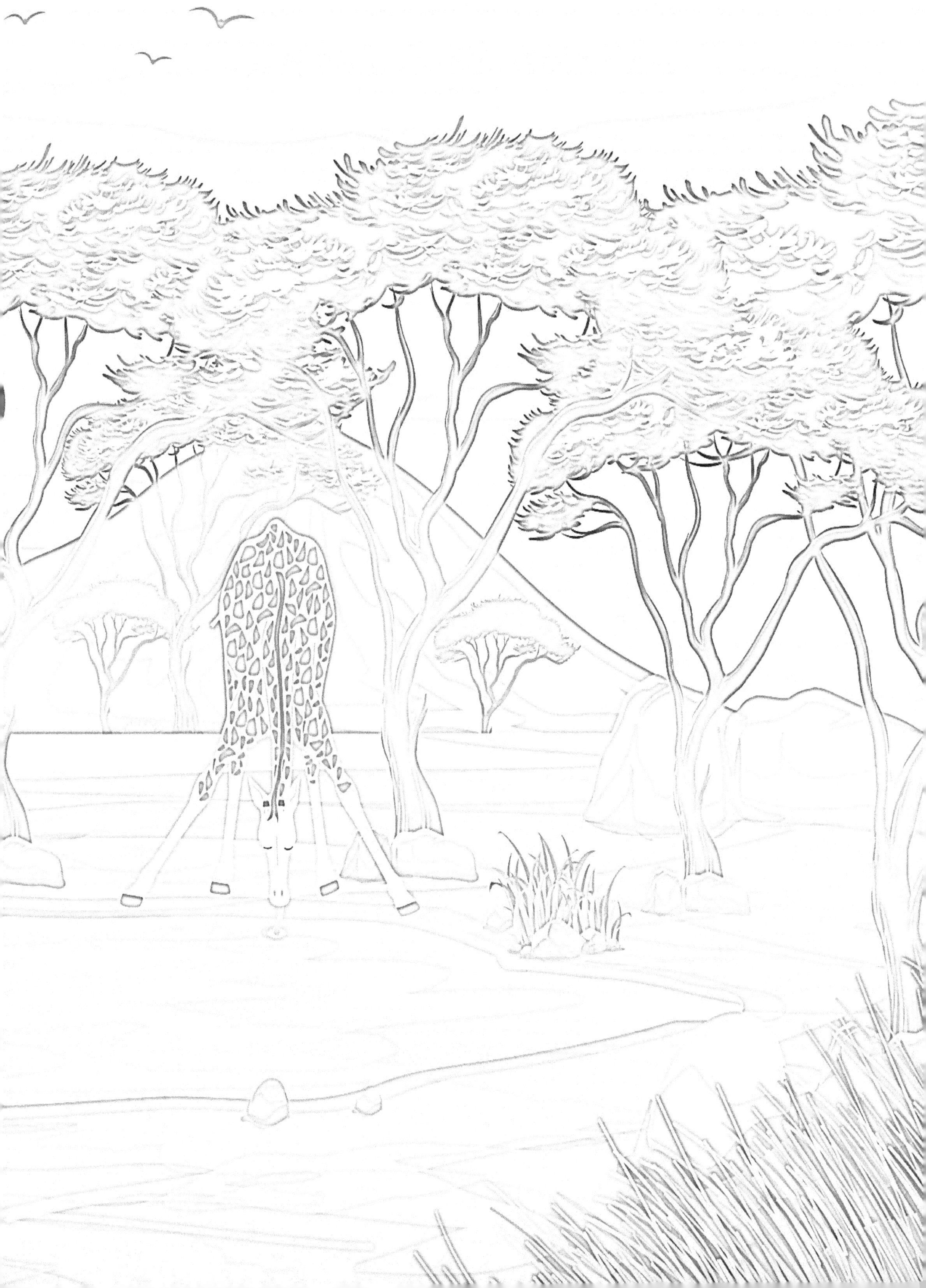

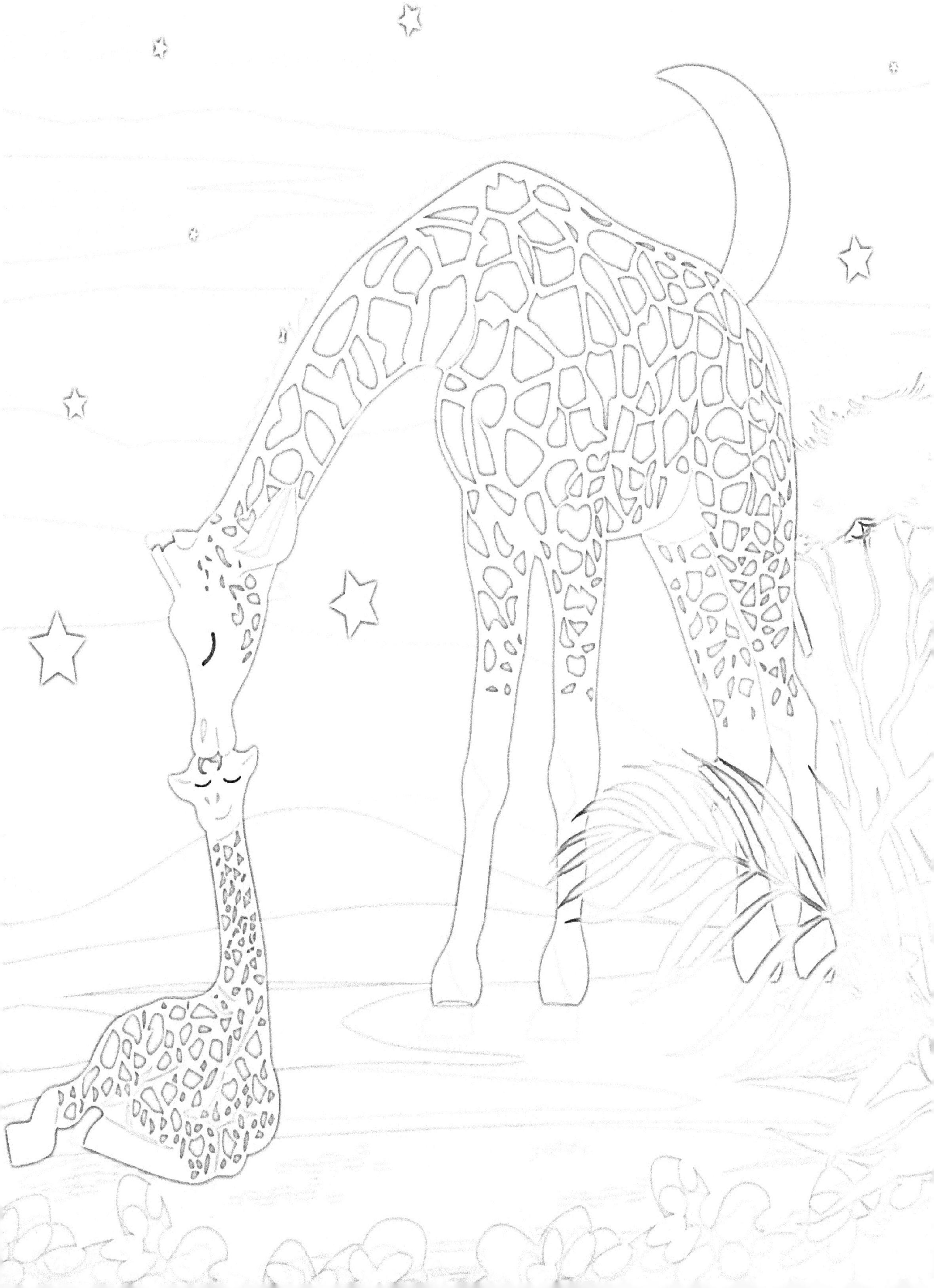

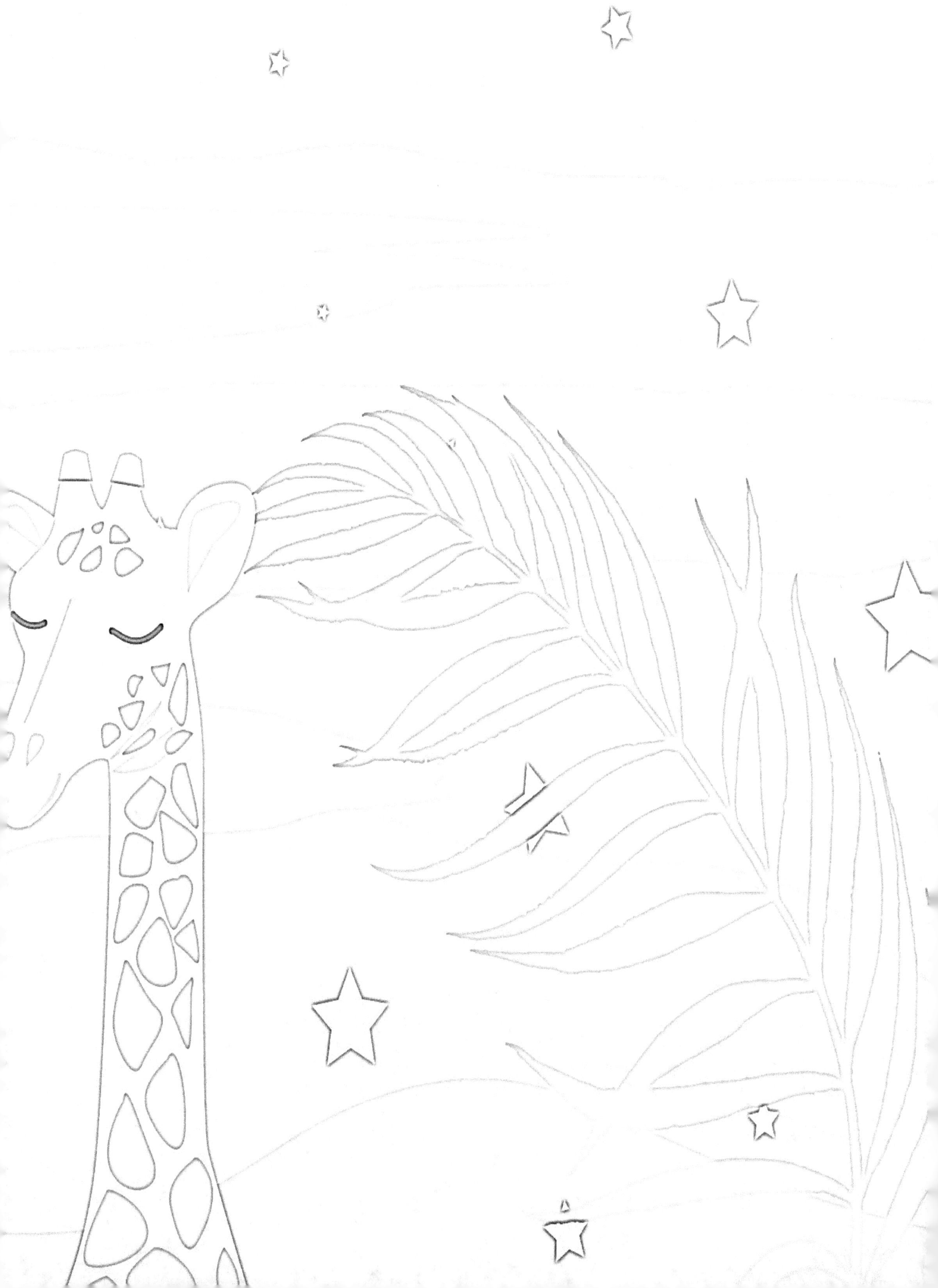

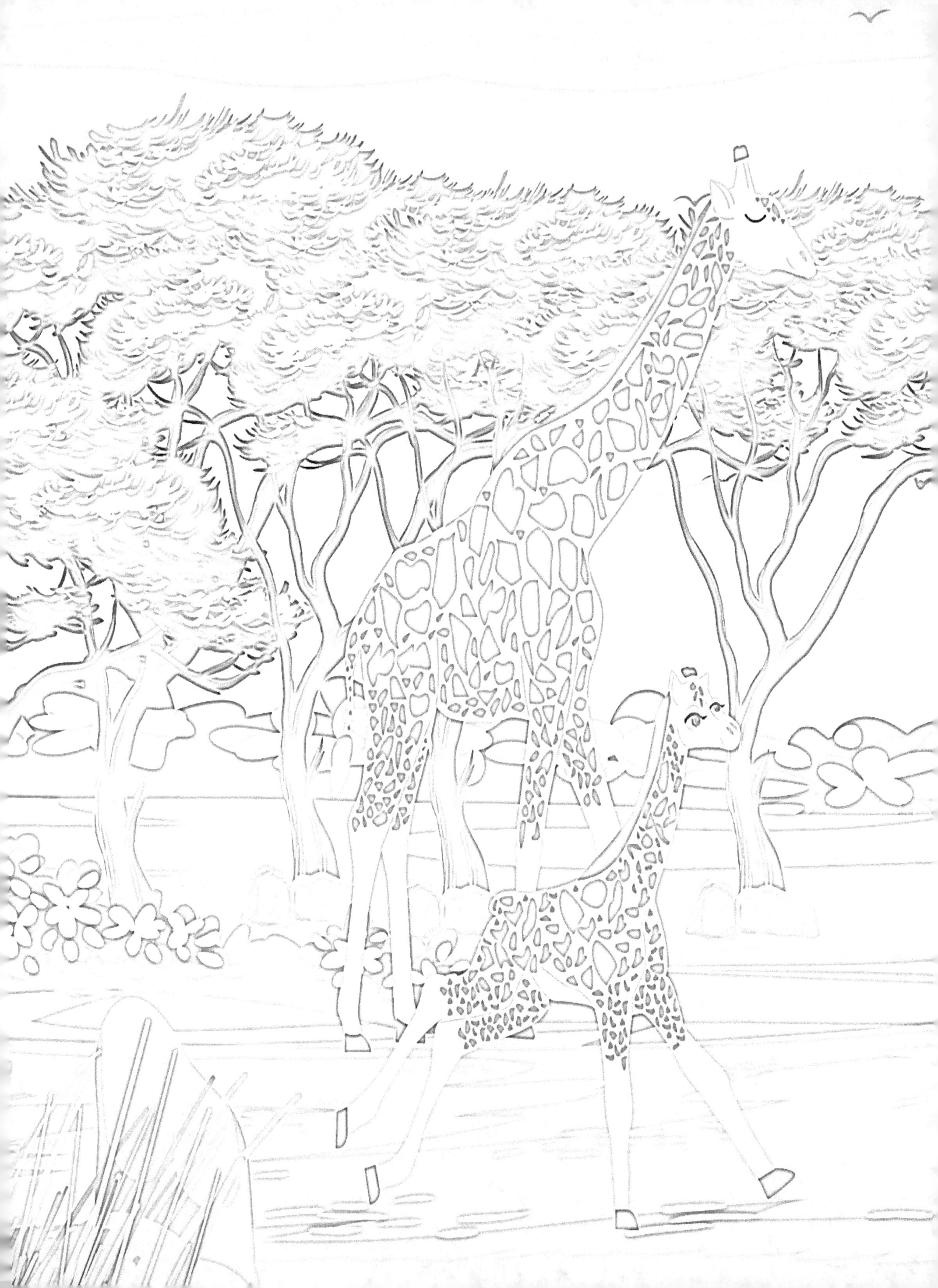

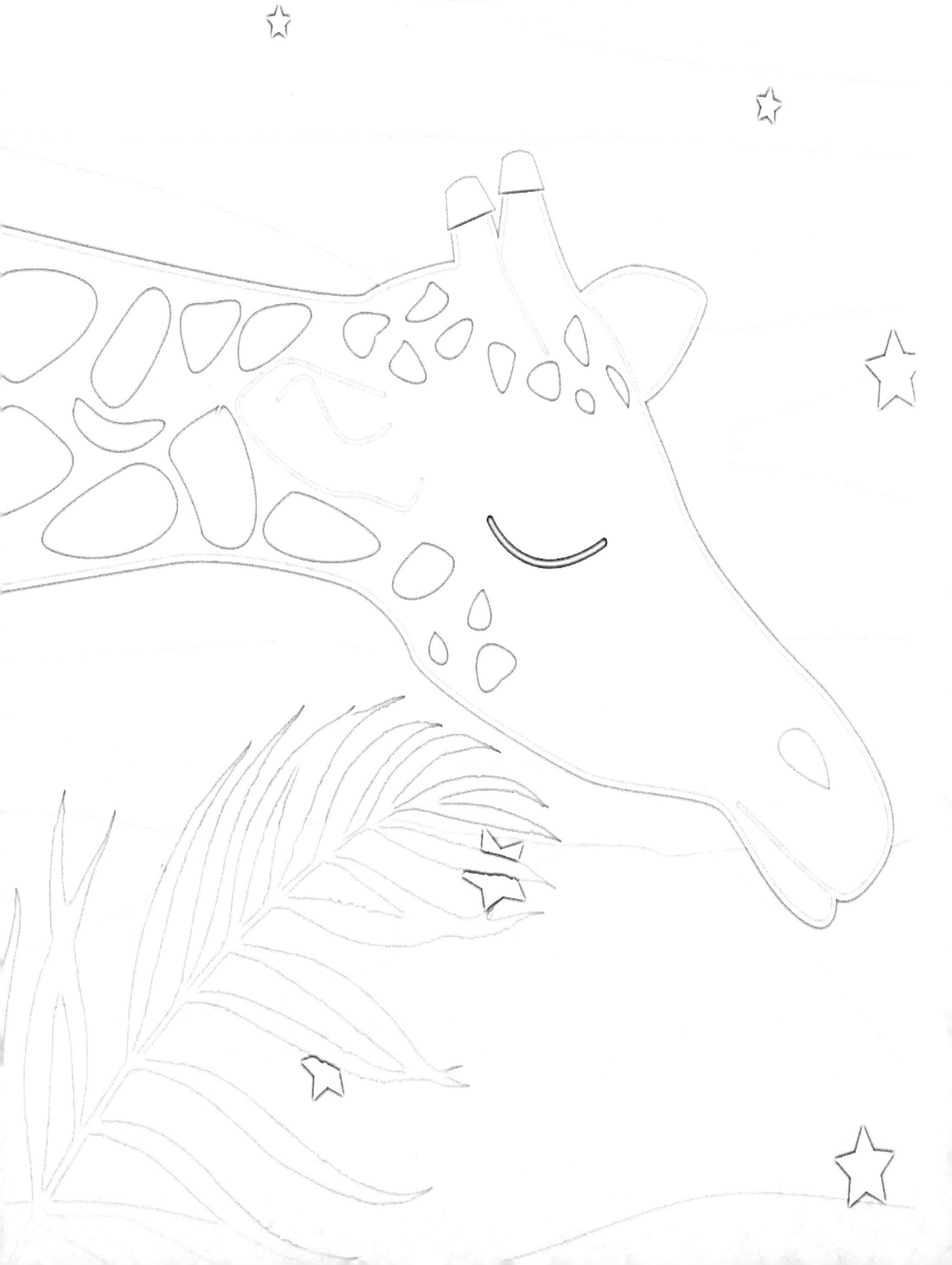

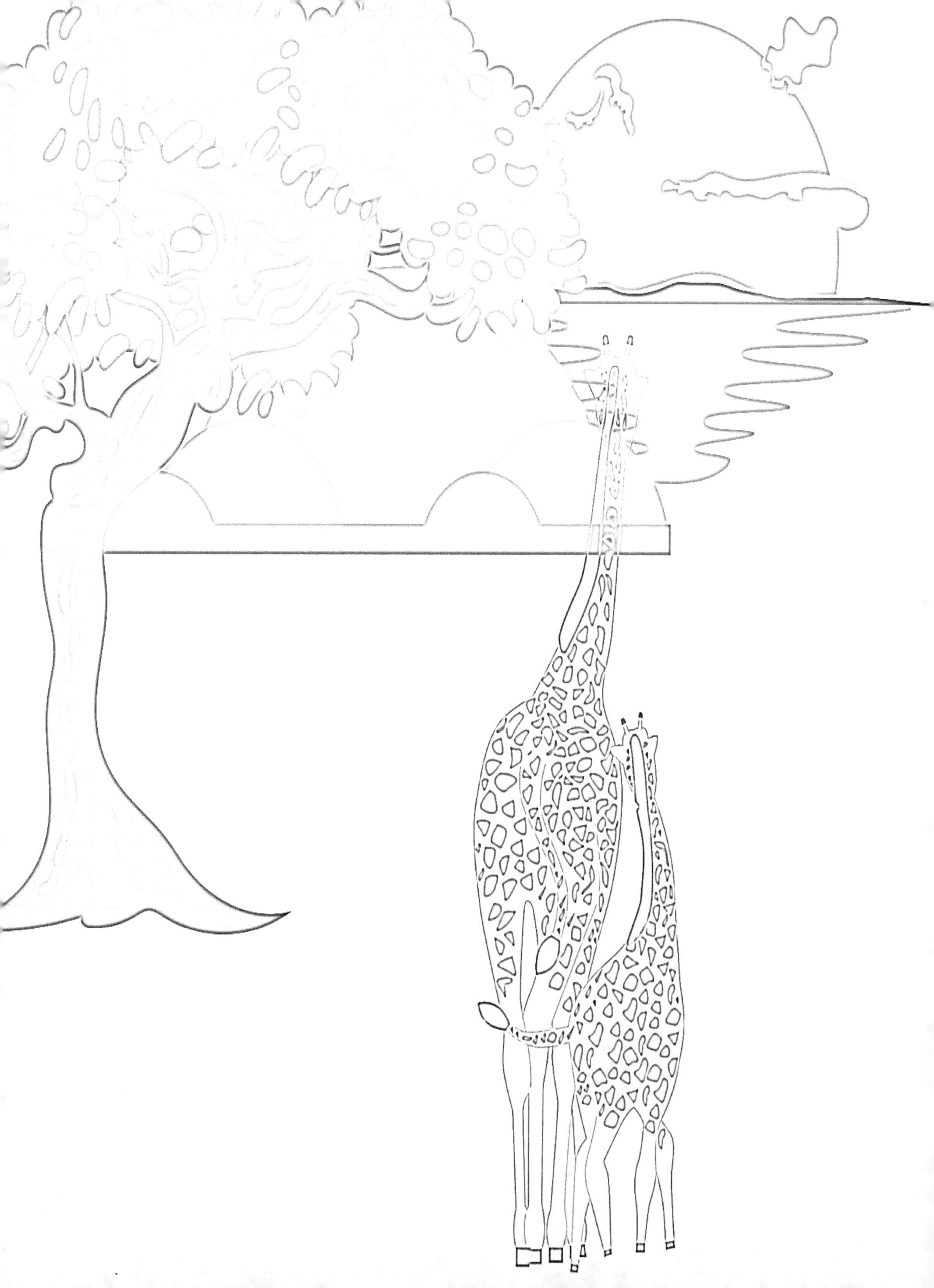

www.ingramcontent.com/pod-product-compliance
Lightning Source LLC
Chambersburg PA
CBHW081458220526
45466CB00008B/2700
* 9 7 9 8 5 2 6 2 2 7 1 4 8 *